Scandinavian Studies
in Criminology, Vol. 9

The Snow-White
Image

Scandinavian Studies
in Criminology, Vol. 9

The Snow-White
Image

The Hidden Reality of Crime in
Switzerland

Flemming Balvig

Translated by Karen Leander

Norwegian
University Press

The Scandinavian
Research Council
for Criminology

Norwegian University Press (Universitetsforlaget AS), 0608 Oslo 6
Distributed world-wide excluding Scandinavia by
Oxford University Press, Walton Street, Oxford OX2 6DP

London   New York   Toronto
Delhi   Bombay   Calcutta   Madras   Karachi
Kuala Lumpur   Singapore   Hong Kong   Tokyo
Nairobi   Dar es Salaam   Cape Town
Melbourne   Auckland

and associated companies in
Beirut   Berlin   Ibadan   Mexico City   Nicosia

Hvid som sne. Kriminalitet og kontrol i Danmark og Schweiz
© Flemming Balvig and Forlaget SOCPOL 1987

English translation © Universitetsforlaget AS 1988

British Library Cataloguing in Publication Data
Balvig, Flemming
    The snow-white image: the hidden reality of crime in Switzerland.—(Scandi-
    navian studies in criminology; v. 9)
    1. Switzerland. Crime
    I. Title II. Series III. Hvid som sne.
    English
    364'.9494

ISBN 82-00-07472-2

Printed in The United Kingdom
by Page Bros (Norwich) Ltd.

Contents

Preface

If through their research criminologists aspire to be useful to society—and in one sense or another of the word useful I think they do—one ought to consider whether criminologists are put in the right place and selected according to the right criteria. Criminologists are generally placed—and conduct their research—where society exhibits its most negative and unhelpful aspects in regard to preventing and fighting violence, theft, vandalism, etc. There are more criminologists in the USA than in Europe, more in the European metropolises than in the countryside, usually more men than women, and more young than old people.

Even when criminologists *are* put in the right place and *are* selected in a proper way they often fail to make good use of their position. The criminology of females becomes the study of the abuse of women and the exploitation of the female sex, and not a forthright and sharp rebellion against a society that fails to make use of strong female cultural traits like sensitivity, creativity, understanding and tolerance for which the society does have a potential, and which are really needed in society, especially from a crime-preventive point of view.

The criminology of old people—if a discipline of this kind can be said to exist at all—becomes a description of weak, powerless and anxious citizens and not the cultural challenge it could be of a society that gives first priority to materialism and a hasty tempo in life. Older women in the countryside are thus the real—the best, the true—experts of crime prevention. They constitute a group in the Western societies which presents the most concrete and enlightening practical example that it *is* possible to exist without being violent, without stealing, without polluting, without vandalizing, etc. They have more to offer in this respect than any other group in society.

Young men in US metropolises represent the opposite pole. They have absolutely nothing to offer when it comes to crime prevention—only a vision of horror. But where do criminologists go when they choose their area of research and the places to which they travel? It is my experience that many more go to the young men in American metropolises than to the old women living in small villages—either literally or indirectly through the journals, papers, books and other things they read. Or more precisely, when we as criminologists want to be *professional*—when we want to learn something about how to behave in a way that does not trigger violence, stealing, robbing etc.—then we literally or indirectly go to the violent, fraudulent, thievish men in the American metropolises. On the other hand, when we just want to be human beings, to be *private*—when we personally want to be treated caringly, lovingly and pleasantly by people who really worry about us, listen to us, and spend time with us, we turn to our grandmothers on the so-called periphery of society. Basically this exposes a widespread alienation among criminologists—a deep disruption which has its roots in, among other things, the positivistic ideal of social science, with its insistence on total separation between the objective and the subjective, the professional and the private.

When we bring up our children we don't do this by asking them to spend as much time as possible together with other children whom we least of all want our own children to emulate, for the purpose of teaching them something about their opposites. But when we try to bring up society, this is the strategy we employ.

The point here is very simple: criminology must study areas and population groups where crime does *not* exist. It is here—practically speaking—that there is most to study and most to learn. A criminology that implicitly or explicitly aspires to prevent crime is best off when studying respect for the law instead of disrespect for the law. Maybe many criminologists agree with this, but then just look at the tables of contents in a few of the most well-known criminological journals and see what criminologists in fact spend their professional time doing.

There are other important reasons for orienting criminology more towards conformity than deviance, but this should suffice for presenting *the rationale* behind this book: it is a book concerned with the law-abiding as a means of gaining new insights into the non-law-abiding.

This is an uncommon approach, but this is not the first criminological work with conformity as its general orientation. It is not even the first book to focus on the *concrete* subject that has been chosen: Switzerland—the country that the American criminologist Marshall Clinard put on the criminological map of remarkable places in 1978 with his book, *Cities with Little Crime*. In this book Clinard claimed that Switzerland distinguishes itself from other prosperous and highly industrialized Western societies by its low criminality. Switzerland thus appears to be one of the few geographical grandmothers left among the highly industrialized and urbanized Western societies.

This book then takes a look at the seemingly exceptional Swiss social structure, at the scope and development of criminality as a product of this structure, and at the Swiss method of dealing with problems of crime—but with the ultimate goal of attaining a yardstick, a suitable mirror-image of, and a competitive alternative to what is, in my opinion, a bogged-down, ritualistic, and ineffective criminal policy and method of crime prevention in countries like my own, Denmark, and most other Western countries.

The book has turned out very differently from what was originally intended because, after a closer look, the *problem* turned out to be different. This book has become more concerned with how we relate to crime than about how we reduce it—which is not a less important matter, just a different one. The conversion of the problem reached in the analysis has also meant that the book is more critical and less 'positive'—more structural and less mechanical, more sociological and less criminological—than first planned. It should be stressed that the criticism contained herein is not aimed at individual *persons*, but rather at certain ways of *studying* and certain ways of *forming* society.

For the fact that the book has come into being, I owe a debt of gratitude to many institutions and individuals.

First of all, I am indebted to the Council of Europe for awarding me the criminology stipend which made it possible for me to spend the month of February 1986 at the Institute of Criminology, University of Zürich. The Social Science Research Council in Denmark has also kindly supported the study financially.

Next, I am grateful to the University of Zürich and its Faculty of Law for the space and facilities they put at my disposal.

I should like to extend special thanks to Cloudio Faoio, Reinhard Frei, Günther Kaiser, Martin Killias, Christian Schwarzenegger, Heinz Stadler and Renate Walder—all of Switzerland—for their help and professional stimulation. I also wish to thank Karen Leander for her diligent translation.

Copenhagen, January 1988

Flemming Balvig

1

In Search of a Land of Little Crime

Criminology derives its sustenance from deviance, but in such a way that it depends both too much and too little on deviance for this sustenance.

When criminology views the search for deviance as the be-all and end-all of its discipline, it is only half alive. Criminology must also search for the *absence* of deviance. It is just as important for understanding the meaning and character of deviance to ask why deviance does not exist as to ask why it does. Criminology should not only concern itself with big cities, men, young people, the USA or other 'crime-intensive' areas, but also with the elderly, women, sparsely populated areas, and countries with little crime. When, for example, the question is raised whether crime and deviance can be prevented, it is important to recognize that women have more to offer men, rural areas have more to offer cities, and low-crime countries have more to offer high-crime ones, than vice versa.

This lopsided concern with crime-intensive areas results in the over-criminalized picture of the world that criminologists work with and convey to others. In the criminological view of the world young persons are transformed into juvenile delinquents, big cities into centers of crime, and streets into settings of random violence, despite the fact that crime is rarely the dominant feature of the persons, groups, or societies being studied. Another consequence is that criminology is afflicted not with bad theories, but with theories that are too 'good'. Theories that explain too much crime in relation to what reality has to offer. For example, in relation to most theories on juvenile crime, we should expect a much higher youth crime rate than is actually the case. Criminology needs to decriminalize its view of the world in order to describe and locate criminality more appropriately within its social context. It is a desirable, or even necessary, step in this process to focus on that part of reality which compels criminologists to try to answer the question: why is there no crime, or why isn't there much more crime than there actually is?

Viewed from another angle, deviance is a necessity for criminology. In all scientific work, deviance—in the sense of exceptions—is of invaluable importance for the production of knowledge. Even if the task of science is to find constant contexts and structures, the advancement of knowledge is still dependent on its seekers keeping a constant eye open for deviations from established theories and ideas. If one advances a hypothesis that alcohol and violence are closely related, our knowledge is not enhanced by information about a society or community where circumstances concur with this hypothesis. Meeting and analysing exceptions and deviations such as societies with negligible violence but widespread alcohol consumption, or the reverse, is much more fruitful for research. In fact, I believe that 'analyzing of deviations' is the most important scientific means for testing and understanding established hypotheses and contexts as well as for promoting the emergence of new frameworks of understanding.

In sum, it is important and productive for the advancement of knowledge and for crime prevention to steer criminological research towards areas with low levels of crime, away from high-crime areas, and especially towards areas of low crime where this low level is unexpected, that is, where it is not compatible with existing theories.

We know that on a national scale, the total level of crime is closely related to the level of affluence and industrialization. The higher the material prosperity and degree of industrialization, the higher the level of theft, vandalism, and violent crimes. The 'deviant' question is then whether it is possible to find examples of countries where, despite wealth and advanced industrialization comparable to that found in, for instance, Scandinavia, there is both an absolutely and a relatively low level of crime.

Most of the countries in the world with little criminality—such as China, Japan, and Saudi Arabia—have such different economic structures, forms of government, cultural traditions, and histories, that, from a shortsighted practical point of view, they are rendered less interesting as possible sparring partners in the field of criminal policy. The ideal here is a country so similar to Denmark in other aspects that it should also be similar with respect to criminality. In other words, we are on the lookout for a crime-prevention sparring partner than can function in the same titillating and challenging way that Holland has done for many years in the field of criminal policy.

Switzerland as a Land with Little Crime

'It is remarkable, but true, that there is almost no crime in Switzerland'. This statement is found in the Danish version of the best-selling guidebook about Switzerland (Berlitz, 1978).

It is not only guidebooks for tourists which convey an image of Switzerland as a corner of the world that is almost free from criminality. Similar images are also found in the existing criminological literature dealing with this Alpine country, in particular in a book by the American criminologist Marshall Clinard, *Cities with Little Crime. The Case of Switzerland* (1978). Clinard's book came out in 1978 but is primarily concerned with the crime situation in Switzerland prior to and during 1973. After a survey of crime statistics, insurance statistics, crime reportage in the media, political debates, and after carrying out his own studies, Clinard felt justified in declaring that it was remarkable, but true, that criminality in Switzerland was low and did not follow the rising trends found elsewhere. What was strange in Clinard's eyes was that we could expect the opposite to be true, taking the country's level of prosperity and degree of industrialization into consideration.

The most recent scientific confirmation of this image of Switzerland as a country of little crime is given by another American criminologist, Freda Adler, in her book *Nations Not Obsessed with Crime* (1983). In this analysis, Switzerland is ranked as one of the ten countries in the world with the lowest rates of crime.

Despite various criticisms of parts of Clinard's and Adler's works, their central conclusion that Switzerland is a country with little crime has not faced serious criminological, scientific resistance or challenge. On the contrary, Clinard's book has virtually become a classic within the field of criminology and has been called a milestone in comparative criminology and acclaimed for being extremely well-documented (see for example, Peck 1979 and Baldwin 1982). Even Swiss criminologists (those few who exist) seem to have accepted this conclusion, not only as a description of

Switzerland at the beginning of the 1970s, but also as a telling portrayal of Switzerland in the 1980s (Kaiser 1985; Killias 1985).

There are also other remarkable but true circumstances surrounding Swiss criminality: for instance, the absence of police statistics, which is the most commonly used indicator within criminology elsewhere of the level and development of crime. Switzerland is not among the many countries about which Interpol collects and publishes annual figures on reported Penal Code crimes. Its neighboring countries—Austria, West Germany, France, and Italy—are all represented, but not Switzerland. For this reason, it is much more difficult for Switzerland than for most other countries to confront (mis)conceptions about the range of and trends in criminality with real data.

Convictions in Switzerland

On the other hand, conviction statistics for crimes against the Penal Code have been collected and published for at least 50 years. These

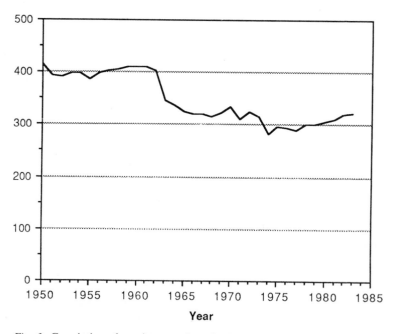

Fig. 1. Convictions for crimes against the Penal Code in Switzerland per 100,000 inhabitants 1950–83

are the country's only, and thus most important and most frequently used, source for describing and interpreting the crime situation.

Convictions for crimes against the Penal Code are remarkably stable. Throughout the entire post-war period, the absolute number has hovered around 20,000, and any fluctuations are conspicuously small and few in number. For Fig. 1, convictions for Penal Code crimes have been adjusted for population from 1950 and onwards.

Up to the early 1960s, the number remained constant at about 400 convictions per year per 100,000 inhabitants. Thereafter, however, we see a drop—for the same period for which most other European countries see a rise. From the end of the 1960s until the 1980s, convictions lie around 300 per year per 100,000 inhabitants.

Convictions in Denmark

More disputable here is whether the total number of convictions for Penal Code crimes is really so remarkably *low*. Clinard does not compare the court statistics for Switzerland with those of any other country.

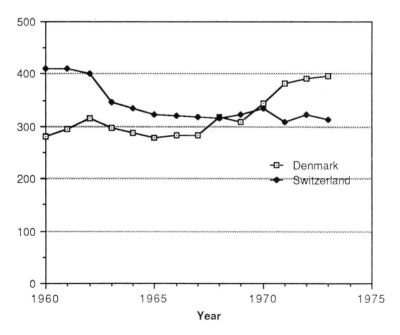

Fig. 2. Convictions for crimes against the Penal Code per 100,000 inhabitants in Switzerland and Denmark 1960–73

To remedy this, conviction statistics for Switzerland are compared in Fig. 2 with the Danish ones for the same period that Clinard studied, that is, from 1960 to 1973. The figure shows no overall difference in the level of convictions between the two countries. Until 1967, Switzerland showed higher values than Denmark; from 1971, the reverse is true. In addition, waivers of prosecution are included in the Danish figures, whereas they are not included in the Swiss statistics. Although less so than in Denmark, waivers of prosecution are used in Switzerland to some degree, especially in the French-speaking region, despite the lack of relevant statistics.

Recent Developments

If we take a close look at Fig. 1, it becomes evident that some changes have occurred since Clinard's study in 1973. If the trend in convictions was a decreasing one until 1973, it is followed by a rise in 1973. Although this increase is not very sharp, it *is* an increase.

There are additional factors indicating that the otherwise stable Swiss society has undergone recent changes, even in areas that could be expected to affect criminality. For example, there are some obvious signs of changes in the level of conflict and of changing values and moral norms.

Changes in the rate of divorce are in part a measure of changes in values and morals concerning the family and in part a measure of the dimensions of conflicts in primary relationships. This rate has risen substantially since the end of the 1960s, as seen in Fig. 3. There it is first of all changes in the divorce rates that push the curve upwards and not changes in the number of marriages contracted.

The number of registered sexual crimes, numerically dominated by offences against public decency, is sometimes used as an indicator of the degree of (sexual) intolerance. As is seen from Fig. 4, convictions for sexual crimes per 100,000 have decreased considerably since the end of the 1960s.

If we compare the trends in divorce rates with those in conviction rates for offences against public decency, it is striking how they rise and fall at the same pace and at the same points in time.

Switzerland is famous for its political stability and its peaceful labour market. But even in these areas there seems to have

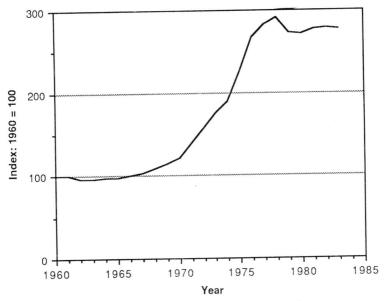

Fig. 3. Divorces per marriages contracted

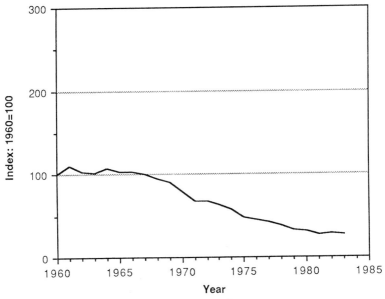

Fig. 4. Sexual crimes
Convictions per 100,000 inhabitants

occurred a radical change since the late 1960s and early 1970s. Attempts have been made to count the 'political incidents' in the Swiss society from 1945 to 1978. By 'political incident' is understood collective action whereby private citizens, not professional politicians, try to influence the events around them (Kriesi, 1981).

Fig. 5 shows the development in the number of 'political incidents' from year to year. There has been a striking increase since the end of the 1960s. Nearly two-thirds of the incidents took place during the last 10 years of the period under study, from 1968 to 1978. A closer analysis of the occurrences shows, however, that it is increasingly a matter of a radicalization as well, both as to the more radical stances taken on the issues and as to the more violent expressions these stances take.

A rather hasty review of Clinard's documentation and an equally hasty look at the development since his study in 1973 thus lead us directly to the following questions: Is it really true that Switzerland was a country with little crime in the early 1970s and/or has so much happened since then so as to invalidate this depiction?

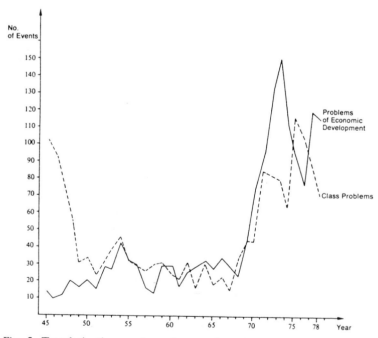

Fig. 5. Trends in the number of events based on problems caused by economic development and class problems

2

The Art of Making Comparisons

Comparative studies can never be divorced from the cultural backgrounds of the societies involved so we must try to bring out these cultural backgrounds onto a *conscious* level.

Nor can comparative studies ever be totally *exhaustive* (just exhausting!), so as to take all relevant dimensions relating to the problem being studied into consideration, but at least we have to try.

Moreover, comparative studies can never be entirely *symmetrical*, that is, based on equally thorough studies of each of the units of measure, but at the very least this must be our aim.

Cultural consciousness, systematization, and symmetry are basic—and simple—*ideal* rules for making comparative studies. Just as they are standards that most comparative studies do not live up to, especially when entire nations are being compared. Unfortunately, in my opinion, Clinard's study is no exception.

The American Perspective

Clinard's book about Switzerland as a country of little crime is unmistakably written by a person rooted in the American culture and life-style. His conclusions and interpretations must be seen against this background. The American perspective clearly filters through some of the rather mundane observations he makes from his stay in Switzerland and which he uses as indicators of low levels of crime. Clinard here describes how he often observed the Swiss leaving their laundry out to dry. He noticed that in apartment complexes, the outside doors were not locked, and that many people went away on holidays or for longer periods without renting out their homes or arranging for their supervision. He describes how Swiss drivers were first compelled to install steering wheel locks in their cars as late as in 1971, and how it was possible to leave a car near a bus-stop for many hours without any great risk of it being stolen. The biggest surprise for Clinard was that Zürich trams have random rather than systematic ticket controls.

None of these observations made by Clinard would be startlingly strange to *Danes*. They describe modes of conduct that Danes, with their Scandinavian background, would hardly notice, let alone pay much attention to, since they do not differ from what people in Denmark do.

But in the light of the crime rates prevailing in the USA, especially for violent crimes, it should probably not be very surprising that Clinard experiences and perceives criminality in Switzerland as relatively low.

One might be justified in asking whether any American criminologist would not in fact reach the same conclusions *no matter what other country was being studied*. If Clinard had instead visited England or the Netherlands or West Germany, for example, I dare say that his conclusion would have been the same.

To some degree, Clinard is aware of this and attempts to compare the situation in Switzerland with that in the Scandinavian countries, primarily Sweden, and with that in West Germany.

The method Clinard uses to make his comparisons, however, is not systematic. Some crime rates are compared with the German ones, others with the Swedish statistics, and still others with those from Denmark. This makes it impossible to evaluate the validity of his *general* conclusion that the Swiss crime rates are, on the whole, lower and have risen less than in other affluent industrialized countries.

It is also the case that Clinard did not make the same efforts to understand the character and background of the figures he uses from the other countries as he did for those from Switzerland and the USA. This means that several of the comparisons cannot withstand close scrutiny. For example, the only two comparisons he makes with Danish conditions are completely misleading.

In one case, a victim survey conducted in Zürich is compared with one conducted in Copenhagen. Clinard finds that 2.5 percent of the interviewees in Zürich claimed to have been assaulted during the previous year. Clinard compares this with a corresponding rate in Copenhagen that he sets at 9 percent. But this is not a valid comparison because the Copenhagen study covers a two-year period and the Danish questions encompassed a much broader definition of violence than just being 'assaulted'.

In the other case, Clinard tells us that 5.8 percent of the inhabitants of Zürich had been victims of personal theft, and he goes on to tell us that a corresponding study in Copenhagen established a theft rate almost three times as high, namely, 15 percent. What he does not mention is that the Copenhagen study included *all* types of theft. When this is taken into consideration, the theft rates become higher in Zürich than in Copenhagen.

The Danish Perspective

One way of challenging and estimating the significance of the *American* perspective is to construct others. It was natural for me to test it from a Scandinavian, or more precisely, a Danish perspective. My main purpose in researching and analyzing crime and criminal policies in Switzerland has not been to understand Switzerland, but rather to increase my understanding of Denmark. The question is whether the way in which the Swiss society functions and is developing may contribute to a better insight into these aspects of Danish society, and whether we can make use of this insight—positive or negative—for revising our plans for shaping society and our methods for forming our future.

Beyond the fact that it is natural for a Dane to stress the Danish perspective, consciously or not, there is a sound criminological reason for contrasting Denmark with a country of presumably little crime. In several statistical compilations, Denmark has been presented as a country with one of the highest levels of crime in the world, such as in Interpol's statistic on police-reported thefts (see Fig. 6).

So the crucial question is then whether Switzerland is a country of little crime when seen from a *Danish* perspective? Would a more exhaustive and symmetrical comparison lead to a different conclusion? Criminality has been on the upswing in Western industrialized post-war societies, but the increases do not occur everywhere at the same time and at the same rate. Is Clinard's land of little crime from 1973 just an example of a cultural lag within a general trend, rather than a permanent and unique phenomenon in the light of the situation as we now see it 10–15 years later?

I will try to answer these questions first by re-analyzing Clinard's book and data sets, and then by adding data collected during a stay in Switzerland in 1986.

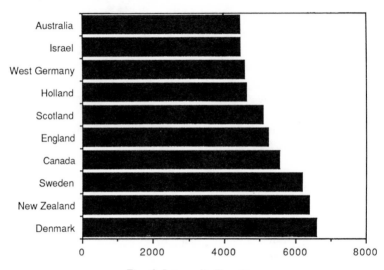

Fig. 6. Interpol's Top Ten
Reported thefts per 100,000 inhabitants in 1982

In contrast, I have not closely examined the more recent analysis of Switzerland as a land of little crime made by Adler (1983). Apparently, Adler did not conduct any independent or, even less so, critical data collection of her own. She relies heavily on other people's information, particularly that of Clinard, so that the strengths and weaknesses of Adler's work are largely identical with those in Clinard's. 'Arrest Rates per 100,000' are used as the main unit of measure for the volume of criminality, and this is found to be 306.7. Adler also uses this figure in her comparisons with other countries and in statistical analyses. Adler seems, however, to have worked under a complete misconception, since a rate of 306.7 would yield an absolute total figure of 18,000–19,000 *arrests*, which is in fact the total for *convictions* for Penal Code crimes in Switzerland. The number of yearly arrests must be at least four times higher.

In addition, it is unreasonable for someone embarking on a new study not to check old figures anew. As for homicide, Adler writes, 'homicide offences are largely a matter for scholarly discussion'. The source of this quotation is an article in a periodical from 1966. On the other hand, she maintains that the crime of prostitution has been taken more seriously. Her source for this statement is another article from 1966. She contends that Switzerland is 'relatively free from problems of poverty or gang subcultures', basing this statement on a study of 100 juvenile delinquents in Geneva in 1965–1966. As for the sentencing system, she claims that conditional sentences are used to a great extent. This is documented with figures stemming from as far back as 1971.

When one is evaluating studies, it is often more important to determine whether the basic figures and information used in the otherwise sophisticated analyses are correct, rather than whether the right formulas, scaling techniques, and so on, are used in processing the basic information. The skills necessary for performing a statistical regression analysis on the basis of questionnaires, for example, are often much more developed than are the skills for writing a good questionnaire, which is really the starting point for it all. The sophisticated statistical processing often serves more as scientific varnish than as a means for expanding our range of knowledge. This is true not least of all for comparative studies.

The Invisible Criminality

Among the basic observations that, intentionally or unintentionally, seem to be important for comparative studies are the researcher's personal and more or less random experiences. Therefore, it is important for these experiences to be discussed openly. As with every other kind of knowledge, it is the first personal and direct impressions that are decisive. It is not easy to convince a researcher who is mugged on his or her first day in a new city that the rate of violent crime there is low. It may be just as difficult to convince a researcher who has lived in an area for months without witnessing any crimes that crime is a frequent daily occurrence in that area.

Criminality is rarely experienced directly. Most lawbreaking activity is not visible. It is quite possible to visit a country for the first time, travel widely, with one's eyes open and all senses on the alert, and still not witness a crime first-hand except for traffic offences. There are two main reasons for this. One is that criminality is a rare occurrence. The other is that it is a kind of activity that the perpetrator in most cases tries to conceal.

The invisibility of crime in daily life makes it necessary to forsake the pulsating vitality of everyday life and retreat to the world of libraries and statistics. It is here that one has the chance to get a general and systematic idea of this uncommon and hidden reality and to find out whether that part of reality in a given place is more uncommon and hidden than in other places.

On the very first day of my stay in Switzerland in February 1986, I found that access to the rooms where this rare and hidden reality was to be discovered and studied was not as direct and easy as might otherwise be expected in a land of little crime.

The relevant statistics were located at the library of the Recht-wissenschaftliches Seminar der Universität Zürich, The Faculty of Law at the University of Zürich. Following a rash of earlier thefts, one's overcoat and bags must be locked in a private box before one is allowed to enter, and then one has to pass surveillance by a guard in a glass booth.

To get to the work room at the modest hotel where I was to analyze the collected information, the main door had to be opened with a key to enter the reception area, and between the main door and the work room there were numerous signs warning the visitor about hotel theft.

There is nothing extraordinary, of course, about these simple measures for combating library and hotel thefts. But it is easy to be astonished by them in a country where it is 'remarkable but true' that there is almost no crime.

Personally I have had one other similar surprise, but one that was of an opposite nature. Together with some colleagues, I once conducted research in an area reputed to have a *high* crime rate. To our surprise, we experienced no crime during our scouring of the area and found the people living there to be very relaxed under the circumstances.

This type of limited experience reveals the ease with which an area can be labelled and the ease with which these labels can have psychological and social consequences. It is this same mechanism that makes it extremely difficult on the personal level to disperse suspicions in other people's minds against persons acquitted of crimes but relatively easy for guilty people to 'get away with it' as long as they are not convicted. Psychologically, the cliché 'high crime area' is transformed into 'always-crime area'. We have obvious psychological difficulties in dealing with degrees of criminality and of crime risks. Either the risk of being subjected to crime is perceived as small or non-existent, or the risk is regarded as certain or near certain. Either we view a person as a criminal or not as a criminal. The gray area in between, where most people, areas, and nations are to be found, is a statistical abstraction which only with extreme difficulty penetrates an individual's experience of the world. It is an abstract item of information to learn that a country has a *somewhat* higher level of crime than another. Information of this type is presumably stored in our consciousness in the same way that psalms and capital cities are memorized, that is, unconnected to the larger picture and with no sensory or social consequences. It is quite another thing when one chooses to call one country a high-crime country, and another, a low-crime country. Such information is experienced as totalities and influences us on both the sensory and social level.

These types of clichés and the surprises they can lead to can, however, be stimulating for research. I would most likely not have chosen Switzerland as the subject of renewed research, if the conclusions of earlier studies had been that Switzerland has 'a somewhat lower level of crime' than other countries. The attraction to the earlier research lies in the definite statement about it being a land of little crime, and I would probably not have criticized this designation—and the earlier research—if some of my initial impressions had not been so devastatingly contradictory.

Despite the stimulating effects of stigmatization and personal impressions, it must be pointed out that both of these are evidentially worthless. Clichés and personal experiences must always be qualified with the sobering knowledge that crimes do not belong to directly observable everyday experience.

In the same way, we must be cautious about estimating the dimensions of criminality from the visible effects of it. Damaged house fronts, for example, may be a result of conscious destruction or of general decay and/or deliberately poor maintenance. Nor are peepholes, door locks, window grills, and the like, reliable indications of crime. It is risky to use the *possible* consequences of crime, because crime is not always mechanically or directly related to specific consequences.

3

The Forgotten Traffic Criminality

For a systematic and statistical estimation of the level and development of crime in Switzerland, it is a natural first step to take a close look at the statistics that Clinard and others have used as the basis of their analyses—statistics on convictions.

In most countries, statistics on convictions are incomplete. Not all sentences are included. Most commonly, statistics on crimes against the Penal Code are the most detailed and accurate.

This concentration on Penal Code crimes in the statistics has come under criticism in recent years. It has been suggested that for one thing, the crimes punished under the Penal Code are not necessarily the most destructive to a society in terms of economic consequences, and that using them may place too much focus on crimes committed by the poorest and most powerless people in society.

Following an old tradition, however, Switzerland does not limit its conviction statistics to Penal Code crimes, but rather includes all violations of laws with penal clauses.

The text accompanying the Swiss conviction statistics (*Die Strafurteile in der Schweiz*, for the respective years) begins with the totals for convictions, and only after that are the figures broken down according to the various types of laws.

Apparently, neither Clinard nor any of the others who have studied criminality in Switzerland have paid much attention to this fact or assigned it much significance. In my opinion, the design of the Swiss criminal statistics is not a coincidence. It shows in an important way how criminal policy priorities are set in Switzerland.

But we can first try to see whether looking at convictions for non-Penal-Code crimes changes the picture of crime trends in

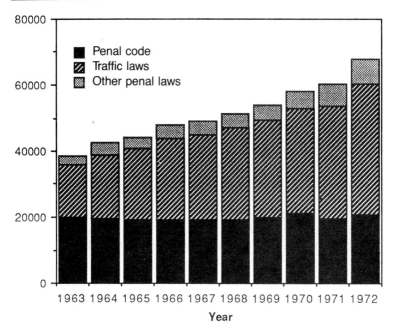

Fig. 7. Number of convictions in Switzerland

Switzerland. Fig. 7 shows the development over the 10 years that Clinard was especially interested in, 1963–1972.

The starting and end points are chosen so that no major statistical reorganizations would interrupt the period studied.

The picture of criminality changes completely. The stability in Fig. 2 is replaced by a clearly rising trend in convictions over these 10 years. It is primarily convictions for violations of the traffic laws that rise, but also other special legislation crimes as well.

In contrast to the early 1960s, the early 1970s were characterized by a yearly total of convictions for traffic law violations that exceeded convictions for all other Penal Code and special legislation provisions combined. Looking at the Swiss criminal statistics for this period, it is striking that the greatest crime problem in that country is traffic criminality.

Again, this is no coincidence but instead a reflection of the fact that traffic offences—and traffic problems in general—are given higher priority within criminal policy in Switzerland than are violence, theft crimes, and so on.

Part of Clinard's study consisted of charting the issues that most troubled the inhabitants of Zürich in 1973. A similar survey was made in Stuttgart, West Germany. Clinard was especially amazed by the fact that criminality came so far down on the list of what people thought were the five most important problems in society. But to me, it is also interesting to note that traffic was clearly regarded as the most important problem and much more so among those responding in Zürich than in Stuttgart.

It is, of course, difficult to reconstruct what the focus of public debate and private worry was 10 to 15 years ago, but it is without question that in February 1986, traffic problems and traffic criminality, on the one hand, were more the subject of concern in Switzerland than in Denmark, and, on the other hand, received at least as much attention in Switzerland as did other crime problems.

There is nothing here that indicates whether traffic problems or traffic criminality are in reality greater in Switzerland than in Denmark, either quantitatively or qualitatively. In fact, the similarities dominate the picture when accident statistics are compared, as well as statistics on persons killed in traffic, studies of drunken driving, and the like. The similarities also seem to dominate for both the levels of crimes and the trends they are following. The small differences found almost all go in the direction of fewer accidents in Switzerland than in Denmark.

The police are organized on the cantonal and municipal levels in Switzerland. Police chiefs are appointed by the city councils and the canton councils. Following each election, the police chiefs and some other high-ranking officers are chosen. Most commonly they are reappointed after new elections. The rank and file police are not civil servants and there is no automatic system for promotions. This system is recognizable from other federal systems and operates to make police activities and police tasks—for better or for worse—more attuned to political sentiments and priorities. So the fact that Swiss police place a much higher value on traffic duty than is the case in Denmark represents a direct consequence of general political opinion.

The usual police patrol cars—personal vehicles with POLICE painted on the sides—are practically never seen patrolling the streets of Swiss cities. Instead, the visible patrols ride in *unmarked cars* which are fitted with equipment intended for traffic control, road markings, speed signs, and so on. Not seldom such equipment fills the back seat that is otherwise used for transporting suspects to jail.

It would not be necessary to drive around Switzerland for long to experience speed-limit controls, vehicle inspections, and/or other traffic checks—either as a witness or as a 'victim'.

Talking to the police soon leaves one with the impression that prevention of traffic crimes and assisting the flow of traffic are viewed as important—and prestigious—assignments. The detective force does not carry the same status as 'the real police', as is typically the case in other countries, including Denmark.

One episode during my stay in Switzerland illustrates in a tragi-comic way how high a priority the police place on combating traffic offences. Five foreign citizens, two of whom were described as dangerous, escaped from a closed prison at Lenzburg. The news of the escape received wide media coverage, being quickly broad-cast on television and radio, and an extensive search was begun. A taxicab was stopped in a traffic control near the St. Gotthard tunnel. One of the escapees was sitting in the front seat and two more in the back. The police carefully examined the car and reproached the front-seat escapee for not having fastened his seatbelt, for which he was fined 100 francs on the spot. The policeman then wished the driver and his passengers well and sent them on their way.

One of the greatest media news items while I was there in February 1986 was the 10 percent decrease in the number of traffic deaths from 1984 to 1985—and the fact that the number had been halved since 1973. This item was given prominent coverage in all the newspapers—with plenty of headlines. Swiss television news programs dedicated about half their air time to this story. The drop in traffic deaths was seen as a result of many years of intense efforts and steps taken, especially on the part of politicians, police, and the highway construction department. In the following month of March, similar statistics were circulated to the Danish media show-ing that from 1984 to 1985 the number of traffic deaths had dropped in Denmark as well by about 10 per cent. No headlines in Denmark splashed this news, and several newspapers did not even run the story. As far as I know, this item was not once mentioned on Danish television news.

The Swiss society has a different relationship to its streets than is the case in Denmark. Traffic in both countries is the cause of considerably more physical damage to the street environment than violence. Traffic, in fact, is ranked rather high on the Swiss citizen's list of personal concerns and has a prominent place in the public debate—which is far from being the case in Denmark. This is a result of two processes, of two more or less conscious choices.

First, appropriations to the police and the way the statistics are constructed and publicized cause public awareness to be focussed on traffic to an unusually high degree. The second factor is one that will be discussed in more detail in the next chapter—that is, the fact that problems of violence and other traditional Penal Code crimes are also pushed, but in this case to the backwater of both the individual and public consciousness.

4

The Juvenile Crime that Disappeared

The rise in registered Penal Code crimes seen in many countries in this century is in large part the product of a rise in juvenile criminality. This applies to Denmark as well.

The development differs so dramatically for the various age groups that many times and in certain periods, simultaneous drops in criminality among adults have been observed.

When the rates for the youngest age groups are both the highest and increasing the fastest, it is obvious that valid comparisons of total conviction rates first of all presuppose complete and uniform statistics on young offenders.

In index form, Fig. 8 shows the trends in convictions of young Swiss offenders for Penal Code violations for the 30 years from 1954 to 1983. The index is based on the absolute number of convictions as they are represented in the official Swiss court statistics (*Die Strafurteile in der Schweiz*, for the respective years).

There is a considerable increase in the number of young persons convicted from 1954 to 1961. This rate then levels off somewhat, only to rise sharply again at the end of the 1960s. A culmination is reached in 1970, at which point the number of convicted youths is more than twice as high as in 1954. This is worth noting, especially in the light of the fact that the total number of convictions remained rather constant throughout the period.

This development can be explained in part by the demographic fact of the growing numbers of young people. But, the rise in the number of convicted youths is much greater than the rise in the number of youths.

The most remarkable part of this trend comes after 1970. As can be seen from Fig. 8, this period is characterized by a dramatic fall

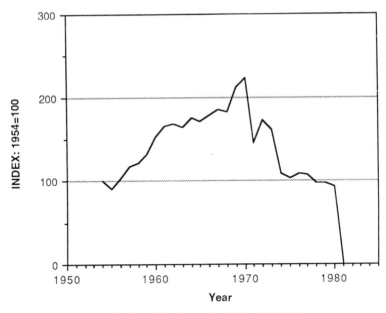

Fig. 8. Trends in Juvenile Crime 1954–83
Number of convicted 14(15)–17 year olds

in the number of convicted youths, especially in 1971, 1974, and 1981. After 1981, juvenile crime stopped! The number of convicted youths in the statistics is 0.

Has Switzerland conquered the problem that no other country has as yet managed to overcome? Has it developed a post-war welfare society without the by-product of increased juvenile criminality?

The answer to this question is that more so than has been done in other countries Switzerland has rendered all trends in juvenile crime in this period *invisible.* Therefore, Swiss Court statistics are unusable as a measure of the scope of and trends in juvenile crime to a higher degree than in most countries.

Crime statistics in Switzerland are based exclusively on information from a central crime register—which is also the case in Denmark. However, not all convictions for Penal Code violations are entered into the register and the reporting criteria have been changed several times. These changes have primarily, but not exclusively, affected juvenile criminality.

In 1954, it was ruled that fines of less than 50 Swiss francs (SF) would not be registered in the Central Criminal Register. Simple theft is an example of a crime covered by this rule. But one should keep in mind here that waivers of prosecution awarded on the basis of the trivial nature of the crime, for example, are only rarely used as an official reaction to crime in Switzerland. Fines therefore have played, and today still do play, a relatively greater role in Switzerland than in Denmark. Simple thefts and minor offences combined are both absolutely and relatively more frequent among juvenile crimes than in adult criminality. Therefore, there is no doubt that even from as early as 1954, the conviction statistics in Switzerland have given an incomplete picture of the total number of convictions, especially those involving juvenile offenders.

Fig. 8 shows that the sharp rise in convicted youths slows down in 1961, the same year that a change was made in the criteria for reporting convictions to the central register. The minimum fine to be reported was raised from 50 SF to 100 SF.

The great drop in the number of convicted youths in 1971 is also related to changes in the registration routines. From the beginning of that year, all juvenile offenders receiving fines have been excluded from the register, regardless of the monetary amount. Moreover, registration of young offenders who had received warnings as a formal sanction was prohibited. The significant reduction in the number of convicted youths by about one-fourth is mainly an expression of the widespread use of fines and warnings in the application of sanctions to youths in Switzerland.

The next greatest drop in the number of convicted youths was seen in 1974. It coincides with the change in the age of criminal responsibility in Switzerland from 14 to 15, so that the statistics from 1974 and onwards refer to 15–17 year olds, while those for the previous years, refer to 14–17 year olds.

There are two ages of criminal responsibility in force in Switzerland: a 7-year limit alongside the 15-year limit. A special fine can be meted out to 7–14 year olds and a special youth punishment to 15–17 year olds. The change made in 1974 entailed an expansion of the penal jurisdiction over children, and throughout the post-war period there has been a rule that sanctions within this juvenile penal jurisdiction are not be reported to the Central Criminal Register. Beyond the implication that crimes by children thus never appear in conviction statistics, this also means in practical, and more essential, terms that convictions of children do not lead to *criminal records.*

Significant for interpreting trends in the total number of convictions is also the fact that in 1974, the limit for registering fines was raised again from 100 to 200 SF.

The very next year, 1975, the registration criteria were changed again. Exempted this time was another sanction applied in juvenile penal law, which most accurately could be said to resemble community service. Furthermore, some conditional sentences were exempted from registration (suspended sentences). Finally, as regards registration of the remaining sanctions, the courts were given the authority to decide which ones would be omitted from the Central Criminal Register. By all accounts, this discretionary power has been increasingly applied by the courts since 1975.

Prison sanctions are not prescribed within the sphere of penal jurisdiction over children and young people in Switzerland. This means that *children and young persons under the age of 18 cannot be sentenced to inprisonment regardless of the type of crime.* However, there is one custodial sanction applicable to young people under certain circumstances and conditions, entitled 'custody', but this sanction is not to be served in prison. 'Custody' may be for a maximum of one year, but very seldom do the sentences even approach the maximum. The minimum is for one day. After the 1975 changes in the registration rules and according to current court practice, very few 'custody' sentences for youths under 18 years are being imposed today or registered in the Central Criminal Register.

The fact that from 1981 onwards young offenders do not appear in the national court statistics at all does not mean that young offenders are not registered anywhere in the Central Criminal Register. Even less does it mean that juvenile crime has ceased to occur. Rather it means that juvenile crimes are no longer included in the national statistics, a clear acknowledgement that these statistics are incomplete.

That the most recently published figures are incomplete in regard to the number of convicted youths is confirmed when the local figures for convictions in juvenile courts from a single canton are compared with the national statistics. I have calculated that only 6–7 percent of such convictions in the Canton of Zürich appear in the national statistics. This concurs well with Kaiser's estimation of 5 percent (Kaiser, 1986).

For several years, there have been plans for designing and producing additional and more comprehensive statistics on convictions of children and young people, but nothing has as yet come of these plans (November 1987).

When one is interpreting the trends in convictions (see Fig. 1), it is important to note that on 1 July 1982, yet another change was made in the registration limit for fines. The limit was raised from 200 SF to 500 SF.

An interesting and essential feature of the history of the Swiss criminal statistics relating to children and young people is that they cannot merely be dismissed as a trivial and technocratic reflection of changed registration criteria and statistical methods. In a more important perspective, I believe they also reflect the special means of dealing with crimes committed by children and young people prevalent in the Swiss society. The invisibility of children and young persons in the official Swiss crime picture is an expression of a strong and widespread reluctance to label as 'criminals' persons who are still developing and learning. The fear is that early labelling may become a self-fulfilling prophecy, whereby children and young people so labelled will seek each other out, and the externally applied label of criminal will be assimilated as part of the personality and identity.

The experience of an American criminologist, Raymond Eve, when he travelled to Switzerland to study criminality among school-children in Geneva (Eve & Cassani, 1984) illustrates this point well. The planned study was intended to test whether the findings from American studies on the causes of crimes committed by children and young persons were sound enough to withstand a confrontation with Swiss reality. The school authorities in Geneva, however, were totally unwilling to allow such a study. The two main reasons given for this decision were, first, that many of the questions were considered as too impertinent and personal; and, second, according to Eve, that:

> . . . the Swiss seem to have a pervasive fear that publicly acknowledging any social problem is not polite and, more importantly, is likely to bring about a self-fulfilling increase in the dimensions of the problem. They appear to be truly concerned that phenomenology implies that they might create social problems by public statements that such problems exist in Switzerland.

Eve drew an analogy between this attitude and sticking your head in the sand and claiming that the danger has disappeared because you can no longer see it. He was also convinced that within only a few years the Swiss would be compelled to allow the question of the growing youth unrest out into the open and discuss it.

It is interesting to note that the labelling perspective has never been theoretically analyzed in Switzerland, but rather has made its main inroads among practitioners and in practical reasoning. The opposite is closer to the truth in many other countries. The labelling perspective plays an important role among researchers and theoreticians there, but a much lesser one among practitioners—and in practice. It is obviously not always the case that a good theory is the basis of a good praxis. Owing to the institutional structure of most societies, it must be admitted that the most insurmountable obstacle to a good praxis is sometimes the development and existence of a good theory.

An immediate consequence of the exclusion of children and young persons from the Swiss criminal statistics is that it then becomes impossible to comment on the development and scope of juvenile crime, and any analysis of the scope and development of the total (Penal Code) criminality is blocked.

Conviction statistics are inadequate as an indicator of criminality, since various selection factors are operating, such as changes in the readiness to report crimes to the police, changes in the willingness of the police to register them, changes in the clearance rates, changes in the prosecution practices, and so on. In the case of Switzerland, I think that using conviction statistics as an indicator of criminality is not only of dubious value, but is in fact completely untenable. There is not the slightest ground for presuming that (Penal Code) criminality has changed in the same way or even in the same direction as the total conviction statistics would indicate.

It should be emphasized in this context that not only have changes in the statistics on young persons occurred over time, but in statistics in general as well. This has especially been the case with regard to raising the financial limits for registering fines. To a certain degree, these changes merely reflect price-index adjustments. But, it is probably also the case that, on the one hand, the sentencing level has been lowered and, on the other, that there has been an increase in those crimes for which relatively small fines are meted out (simple thefts, 'joy-riding', minor property damage, and so on).

One can wonder whether it is possible to find areas within the scope of the conviction statistics that give a more realistic picture of the development of criminality than that seen from the total conviction statistics. I have made three attempts to do just this.

In the first attempt allowance is made for the fact that conviction statistics can only to a very limited degree capture an *intensification* of the crime picture. If an upswing in crime does not primarily consist of a greater number of persons committing criminal acts, but rather of the criminals in question each committing more and more criminal acts, this would hardly show up in the conviction statistics. The post-war period has been characterized by just such a situation in many countries, including Denmark.

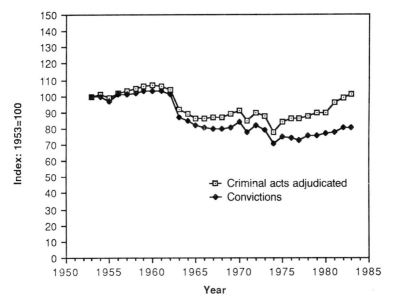

Fig. 9. Convictions and criminal acts adjudicated

It is a little baffling that Clinard did not address this problem, since the Swiss conviction statistics contain material relevant to this question. Conviction statistics thus do not only provide information on the number of convictions, but also on the number of criminal acts adjudicated.

Fig. 9 shows us that the number of offences tried per conviction has risen. The escalation is especially strong after the middle of the 1960s and accelerates in the mid-1970s. There is, therefore, no doubt that the number of Penal Code violations by adults adjudicated has clearly risen in Switzerland since the middle of the 1970s.

The second attempt at using conviction statistics as a more realistic barometer of criminality consists of looking at the development of crimes that—ideally—fulfil the following conditions:

1) high incidence of reported cases, that is, a low dark figure
2) high clearance and prosecution rates
3) deprivation of liberty as the dominant sanction
4) high correlation with other crimes
5) offenders preferably over 18 years of age

The 'ideal' criminal violation for our purposes is thus a crime that, on the one hand, always leads to a court decision and appears in the (Swiss) conviction statistics, 'untouched' by possible changes in the way the statistics are compiled, and that, on the other hand, has been shown empirically to represent only the top of the (crime) iceberg. No such crime exists, but one that comes close is robbery. Manslaughter is another candidate, but manslaughter is not shown separately from other violent crimes in the conviction statistics.

The sole time series on criminality in Clinard's book is in fact, concerned with robbery, for which he presents totals of convictions from 1951–73, the number per 100,000, and an index for this rate. He concludes that the frequency is not only low for this period, but also remarkably stable.

If we compare this with the situation in Denmark, it is not very different. In Denmark the level was somewhat higher, but stability also characterized both the 1950s and the 1960s. The sharp post-war rise first appeared at the end of the 1960s and the early 1970s. Clinard's figures for Switzerland show a corresponding upswing in this period.

In the light of the fact that Clinard did not complete his manu-script until 1978, it is surprising that no totals for robbery—as is true for many of his other figures as well—are updated for the years after 1973. I have looked at the development of robbery convictions since 1973.

Fig. 10 shows an extremely sharp rise in convictions for robbery. The rate of convictions has more than quadrupled from 1970 to 1983, and we can see that the number of adjudicated cases of robberies has risen even more, six-fold. The escalation shown in the general level of crime is thus found for robberies. And the development is identical to the one in Denmark.

The third attempt at finding a more relevant use of the court statistics consists of procuring more complete information on the number of convicted 15–17 year olds. For the largest canton, Zürich, statistics have been available since 1975 on the number of

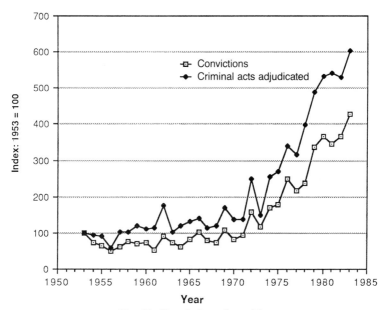

Fig. 10. Convictions for robbery
18 years and older

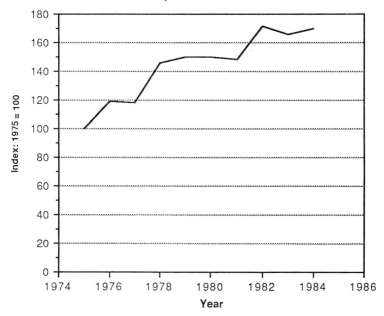

Fig. 11. Trends in juvenile criminality
Penal code convictions, Canton of Zürich

15–17 year olds who have been convicted for violations of the Penal Code, regardless of the type of sanction or whether the case had been registered in the Central Criminal Register. Whereas the national statistics on convictions for the Canton of Zürich show a falling trend corresponding to the one in Fig. 1 for all of Switzerland, the local figures for convicted youths show a clear rise (compare Fig. 11).

The number of convicted 15–17 year olds in the Canton of Zürich has increased by about 75 percent, a rise that can only in small part be explained by the expansion in the size of this age group.

Therefore, it must be concluded that the official crime picture from conviction statistics gives a false and misleading impression of crime trends in Switzerland, not least of all for juvenile crime and for all groups, especially for the period since the early 1970s. A close look at the conviction statistics and how they are compiled has revealed a clear and pronounced rise in Penal Code crimes in Switzerland over the past 10–15 years.

5

The Hidden Statistics

A country's official statistics are an important source for learning about the country. For one thing, we can learn about the conditions prevailing in the country and its organization from the figures themselves and their dimensions. But statistics can also convey *indirect* information, implicit in the choice of which items are to be taken up and which are not, as well as how much space is allowed to various topics, why the statistics are compiled in the way they are, and why some topics are given priority over others. It is hardly a coincidence that in statistics on population trends for—the moralistic—Switzerland, in one and the same table, the number of marriages appears *first*, *next* comes the number of births, and, *last* the number of deaths. In Denmark, figures on marriages entered into are given separately from those on the number of births and deaths.

Nor is it a coincidence that the statistics in Switzerland on *foreign citizens* and the conditions under which they live are comprehensive. All statistics on population are broken down into Swiss and foreign citizens. This variable is often indicated even before sex and age. This is the case with the—sparse—national crime statistics on persons convicted of Penal Code violations. These indicate citizenship, but not age. This focus on foreigners reflects the general importance of the question of citizenship in Switzerland, and it reflects and conveys a picture of an especially strong control and monitoring of foreigners in Switzerland (see Chapter 7 for further details).

It is likewise the case that Swiss statistics are excessively *sparse* when it comes to the question of the *income and financial circumstances* of individuals and organizations. People are reluctant to speak about these topics in Switzerland. If no statistics are compiled on these items, there is less reason or basis for discussing them. The lack of income and capital statistics also reflects the lack of societal control in these spheres in Switzerland, and the flawed statistics reduce the basis for and possibility of systematic and effective control.

Police Statistics

In general, Switzerland produces a wealth of statistics. *Statistisches Jahrbuch der Schweiz* (The Statistical Yearbook of Switzerland) contains substantially more figures than the Danish *Statistisk Årbog* (Yearbook of Statistics), which in its turn is not diminutive compared to other works. So, there is no *general* lack of interest in statistics that would explain the fact that Switzerland neither at the time of Clinard's study in 1973 nor today compiles official statistics on *reported* crimes. However, it has become possible to give a reasonably accurate estimate of reported crimes. A stenciled report entitled *Minimale Kriminalstatistik* has been published since 1982, and it covers all of Switzerland. Reported violations of selected criminal laws are presented, including the numerically significant section on theft crimes. Since 1980, the Canton of Zürich has published computerized total police statistics (*Kriminalstatistik des Kantons Zürich*). The Canton of Aargau followed this example in 1984 (*Kriminalstatistik des Kantons Aargau*), but there are as yet no plans for doing so on a national basis.

It is remarkable in itself that although reasonably accurate material has now been available for 3–4 years with which to estimate the total reported penal violations, no one has taken on the simple task of making these calculations. As has been mentioned, *Minimale Kriminalstatisik* is a stenciled report with limited distribution. The stenciled form contrasts sharply with the bound book form, which is the standard for Swiss publications.

An attempt was made in connection with Clinard's study in 1973 to assess the number of reported Penal Code violations (Kaiser, 1973). This assessment should be regarded as rather uncertain, but one is still surprised that it was given so little attention in Clinard's work. It is no more uncertain than many of the other gauges that were used.

A comparison of Clinard's estimate from 1973 with figures from other European countries shows that the level of crime reported to the police per 100,000 inhabitants was not very high by central

European standards. *But it was not particularly low either.* The three neighboring countries—West Germany, France, and Austria—all fell within the range between the maximum and the minimum estimates seen in Fig. 12. The fourth neighboring country, Italy, was on a much lower level, but police statistics in Italy are notoriously unreliable.

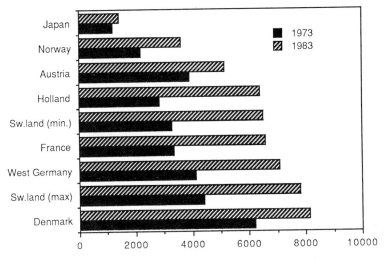

Fig. 12. Penal code violations reported to the police
Per 100,000 inhabitants

Regarded in a Scandinavian context, Switzerland was on a lower level in 1973 than Sweden and Denmark, but higher than Norway and Finland.

Another often discussed industrialized 'country of little crime' is Japan (Kühne & Miyazawa, 1981). The level of reported Penal Code violations in Switzerland in 1973 was much higher than the Japanese level.

If we are now looking at a more accurate estimate—again consisting of maximum and minimum levels—computed on the basis of the available police statistics for 1983, all of the trends mentioned above become even clearer. Seen from a *Danish* perspective, it is noteworthy that Switzerland and Denmark lie on almost the same level. For example, the difference between Denmark and *Norway* in 1983 was considerably greater than the difference between Denmark and Switzerland. The main reason for this lies in the fact

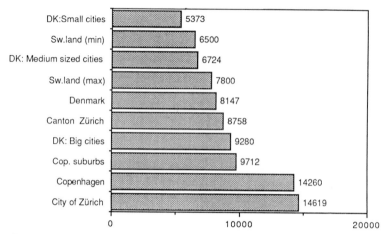

Fig. 13. Penal code violations reported to the police in 1983 per 100,000 inhabitants

that minor offences are not included in the Norwegian figures. Another remarkable fact is that the neighboring country of Austria in 1983 clearly lies on a lower level than Switzerland.

A more detailed comparison of the levels of reported Penal Code violations in 1983 in Denmark and Switzerland is given in Fig. 13. We can see from the figure that the level in the City of Zürich is quite similar to that in the municipality of Copenhagen (*Københavnhavns Politikreds*). Furthermore, the level for the entire Canton of Zürich corresponds rather closely to the level of those police districts in Denmark that are dominated by the bigger cities (Århus, Ålborg, and others).

In any case, that a pronounced rise in traditional Penal Code crimes has occurred since the beginning of the 1970s in Switzerland must be seen as beyond doubt.

Insurance Statistics

Statistics used to supplement or to replace police statistics point in the same direction. *Insurance statistics*, for example, can be used as indicators for theft trends. Clinard spoke with insurance people who did not consider thefts particularly troublesome for the insurance branch. However, it must be remembered that insurance practices in Switzerland are of a radically different nature, especially compared with those in Denmark. Many services or areas that receive public financing via taxes in Denmark are financed via insurance in Switzerland. Taxes are relatively low in Switzerland, but the difference between the two countries diminishes if consideration is given to household expenditure on taxes *plus* insurance. Generally, expenditure on insurance is as great or greater than that on taxes. Many types of insurance are mandatory. It is clear that thefts play a far more modest and less visible role for the total *volume* of insurance in this type of system than in many others.

If we look at the actual figures for theft claims made to insurance companies and their trends, thefts become somewhat harder to disregard. Claims paid for thefts per inhabitant measured in fixed prices doubled from 1960 to 1970. From 1970 to 1983, this figure quadrupled. See Fig. 14.

Payments for thefts made up 4 percent of all insurance claims paid in 1960, 5 percent in 1970, and 10 percent in 1983—see Fig. 15. Clinard makes no use of this type of calculation, but instead uses the size of the premiums paid as an indicator of the dimensions and trends in theft.

Another important indicator that Clinard uses is the ratio between claims paid and premiums paid in. Whereas this pro-

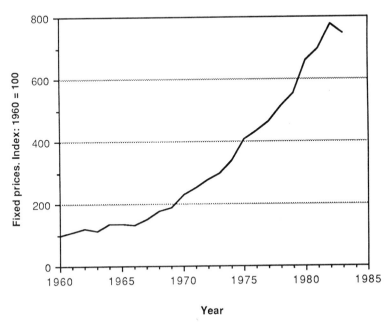

Fig. 14. The value of compensated claims for thefts per inhabitant

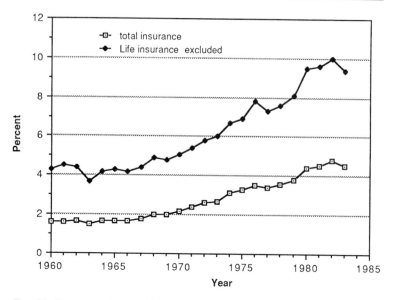

Fig. 15. Compensations paid for theft in percentage of total compensations

portion was between 45–50 percent in the 1960s, it has grown to about 75 percent in the 1980s—see Fig. 16. Interestingly, Clinard quotes an insurance industry standard of 60 percent as the critical value at which thefts become quite burdensome for the industry and of 75 percent as the 'super-critical' limit. The critical limit was already passed in 1974, the year after Clinard's stay in Switzerland, and the 'super-critical' limit had been reached by the start of the 1980s. The introduction in recent years of deductibles in theft insurance, as in Denmark, is a sure sign that recent developments have in fact become a source of concern in the insurance industry. The sharp fluctuations cannot be explained by changes in the insurance coverage.

It is not only the trends but also the levels that are interesting to compare. In 1974, about 100 million crowns were paid out in Denmark in compensation for burglaries. The corresponding figure for Switzerland, corrected for the greater population, was about 120 million crowns, that is, about the same as when the differential price levels between the two countries were taken into account. In 1983, a total of 600 million crowns were paid out in compensation for thefts in Denmark, excluding thefts that are covered by insurance for loss or damage to a motor vehicle. The corresponding

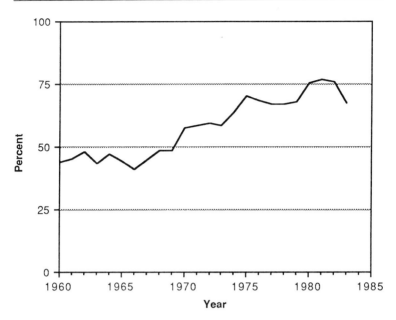

Fig. 16. Compensations paid as percentage of premiums paid in theft insurance

and comparative 1983 figure for Switzerland is more than one billion Danish crowns, that is, about twice as much.

In 1965, the Swiss insurance industry registered about 3.8 reported theft claims per 100 insured persons. In 1972, this figure was 8.5 and in 1977, it was 11.5, in other words, more than one-tenth of all insured persons in one year. This is more than in Denmark.

Statistics on Causes of Death

It is more difficult to find alternative and supplementary statistics for crimes other than theft. According to *Minimale Kriminal-statistik*, there were 92 cases of manslaughter in Switzerland in 1983, which corresponds to 1.4 per 100,000 inhabitants. For Denmark, the figure was 54, which corresponds to 1.1 per 100,000 inhabitants. It is possible that the Swiss legal concept of manslaughter is somewhat broader than the Danish one. If we include all cases of violence ending in death in the Danish figure, the rate for Denmark rises to 1.5.

6

The Hidden Criminality

The traditional and central problem with both police and insurance statistics is that differences and fluctuations may be due to differences and changes in *the readiness to report crimes* and/or *the propensity to register them.*

Victim Surveys 1973

One thing that Clinard deserves credit for is his attempt to cast light on this problem in a concrete way by conducting a victim survey in Zürich in 1973, a study that was directly comparable to a similar one made in Stuttgart, West Germany.

The conclusion that Clinard reaches from his survey and from comparisons with victim surveys in Stuttgart, Scandinavia, and the USA, is quite clear. Clinard concludes that these studies indicate a relatively low level of crime in Zürich.

If the data from the surveys are subjected to closer scrutiny, however, it is difficult to see how this conclusion is justifiable. In Chapter 2, it was mentioned that all comparisons with Danish surveys were misleading and misunderstood. But even if the comparison is limited to the parallel survey in Stuttgart, the conclusion seems unreasonable.

Of the households surveyed in Stuttgart, 32 percent stated that they had been victims of one or more types of crime in a period of one year. For households in Zürich, this figure was 34 percent. Thus, there is *no difference in the total criminality*, and *one may well question the justification of designating as one with little crime an area where almost every third household is victimized yearly by one or more theft, act of vandalism, and/or violent crime.*

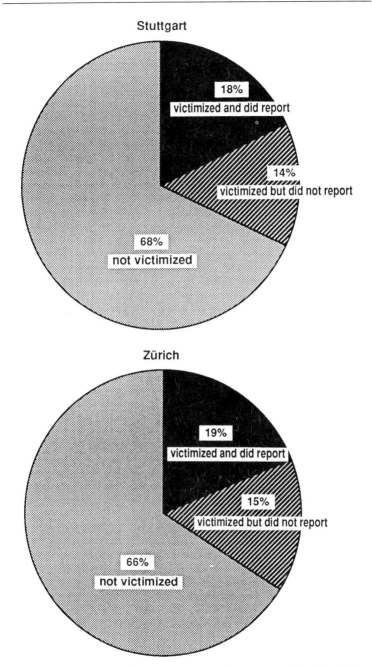

Stuttgart

18%
victimized and did report

14%
victimized but did not report

68%
not victimized

Zürich

19%
victimized and did report

15%
victimized but did not report

66%
not victimized

Fig. 17. Victims of crime in percentage, Stuttgart and Zürich 1973

If we look at three of the most serious crimes dealt with in the surveys—burglary, actual assault, and violent theft—Zürich does not lie significantly below Stuttgart. The rate of violent attacks in Zürich was in fact on a par with that in the American cities of Denver and Portland and significantly higher than in Stuttgart. In Zürich, 8.3 percent of the respondents had been burglarized in the previous year. This figure was 9.6 percent in Stuttgart. Clinard comments upon this difference: 'Burglaries or attempted burglaries per 1,000 households in Zürich were 83, whereas Stuttgart had a considerably higher rate of 96'. Whereas Clinard uses elegant statistics elsewhere in his analyses, here he does not once use even simple significance calculations. Had he done so, he would have discovered that what he calls a considerable difference in the rate of burglaries between Zürich and Stuttgart was not in fact statistically significant, the reason being that only 482 people were interviewed in Zürich, a very small number for victim surveys. Nor does the difference become greater or more significant when the rate is given per 1,000 instead of per 100, even if psychologically it may seem to do so.

Possibly, the level of automobile thefts is somewhat lower in Zürich than in Stuttgart, but it requires some boldness on the part of the researcher to reach this conclusion when the percentual difference is 1.3 percent and when the absolute number of stolen cars in the Zürich study is only 6—4 attempts and 2 completed thefts. Clinard stresses that the numbers are limited and therefore difficult to analyze.

The difference that Clinard is even more interested in when he draws his overall conclusion is the one found for simple theft from private persons outside of their residences, such as bicycle theft, cloakroom thefts, and the like. These are the mildest and least serious crimes covered in the surveys. The rate in Zürich was 3.7 percent and in Stuttgart 6.7 percent. This difference is statistically significant. However, a closer inspection of the two studies shows that comparing just these two rates is not without problems. Thus, it can be stated with certainty that the rate for Zürich is too low. That rate was reached by asking representatives for the households about the experiences of the entire household. In Stuttgart, questions were put both to such representatives of the households and—for a small part of the sample—to all persons in the households. On comparing these two methods, it was found that asking everyone in the household generally led to a crime rate 50 percent higher than when only one respondent answered the questions.

Simply, when all individuals were questioned, many events came to light that were unknown to or forgotten by the household representative. The rate increased especially for *simple theft from private individuals.* The Stuttgart figures that Clinard compares with his Zürich figures are not derived from household representatives, which would have been the correct choice, but rather from all household members. His defence for doing this, in my opinion, is not very convincing: *'The differences between Zürich, on the one hand, and Stuttgart, Denver, and Portland, on the other, are generally so great, however, that this difference in interviewing procedures had little effect on the general conclusions that can be drawn from the comparisons'.* Clinard also finds it important that in Zürich professional interviewers from a commercial market research company were used, whereas students were used in Stuttgart. However, the student interviewers in Stuttgart were described in the German report as *'selected and trained interviewers . . .'* (Stephan 1982).

An interesting question is whether there is any difference in the readiness to report crimes and whether the differences and similarities in the victimization rates correspond to similar differences and similarities in the rates of thefts, vandalism, and violence registered by the police. Clinard does not go any deeper into this question. We must turn to Stephan who conducted the survey in Stuttgart for such information.

Overall, Stephan finds that the reporting percentages are identical for Stuttgart and Zürich. Of the 32 percent who were victimized by crime in Stuttgart, 55 percent said they had reported the crimes to the police. Of the 34 percent who were victimized in Zürich, 56 percent claimed to have reported the crimes. Greater concurrence would hardly be possible to obtain, and consequently we could expect that registered crimes in Zürich and Stuttgart were about on the same levels. But this was not the case. In Stuttgart, 81.5 property crimes were reported per 1,000 inhabitants, and the Zürich figure was only half as great, 45.1. The rates for violence were 2.1 in Stuttgart and 1.0 in Zürich.

Stephan shows that there is a general discrepancy between the number of people who say they have reported crimes and the number of crimes actually registered, but this discrepancy is much greater in Zürich than in Stuttgart and also greater there than in American cities: *'In summarizing the discrepancy between the victimization survey results and the police criminal statistics, one may suppose that the police in Switzerland more easily tend to keep the figures of their crime low, whereas the North American police try to increase as far as possible the police statistics'.*

Clinard is aware of the possibility of differences in police registration practices, but misses the important point about the Swiss police's pronounced tendency to keep criminality out of the statistics. As one reviewer of Clinard's book also pointed out, Clinard is often prepared to accept uncritically viewpoints expressed to him by 'well-informed and important people' (Baldwin 1982). This happens, for example, in the very sensitive area of police registration practices. Clinard writes, *'crimes reported (to the Swiss police), or coming to their attention, seem to be carefully recorded, according to professors of criminal law and various public officials'.* The above-mentioned reviewer makes an apposite comment about this: *'Whatever the merits of professors of law, according them this degree of perspicacity seems scarcely justified'.*

Self-report Studies 1973

The other principal method besides victim surveys for charting total criminality, and determining the proportion of this which is hidden, is self-report studies. Self-report studies are primarily used among children and young persons, who are in fact a group that is of special interest for the problems focussed on here. Clinard states that he regards what he considers to be low juvenile crime rates as one of the major explanations for the overall low crime rates in Switzerland.

In Chapter 4, we questioned whether the *registered* juvenile criminality is as low compared to that of other countries and as static as the conviction statistics would have us believe.

But beyond this, there is a Swiss self-report study whose results also bring into question whether the *total* juvenile crime rate can be regarded as particularly low. This self-report study was conducted in 1973 among 707 young men between the ages of 15–19 in Zürich (Casparis & Vaz, 1978). Clinard does not compare these results with those from corresponding studies in other countries. Instead, he restricts himself to brief comments about the absolute numbers. As to the figures on crimes, he states generally that '. . .—*a large population, ranging from 26 to 86 percent, reported never having engaged in any crimes'.* With equal justification, one could reverse these figures and state that a rather large proportion—from 14 to 74 percent, regardless of the type of crime—reported having committed one or more crimes. As for the most serious crime asked about, namely burglaries, Clinard asserts *'Almost 90 percent had never committed a burglary . . .'* Here, too, the conclusion could be reversed and the statement made that over 10 percent of the young men admitted to at least one burglary. Finally, he claims that: *'Vandalism is perhaps the most typical of all youth offences in western countries. This offence, however, appears not to constitute a major problem in Switzerland'*. In the questionnaire study, however, three-fourths of the young men admitted to having vandalized public or private property, and nearly one-fourth revealed five or more such occasions.

This picture of the crime rates among young men in Zürich in 1973 does not diverge much from corresponding results in similar studies in other countries. For one thing, the findings on burglaries are directly comparable with findings from the studies on conscripts conducted in the Scandinavian countries during the 1960s. The average age among the young people surveyed in the Scandinavian countries was somewhat higher. Whereas 14 percent of the young men in Zürich admitted having committed burglaries, the figure for Copenhagen was 7 percent, Oslo 12 percent, Helsinki 16 percent, and Stockholm 13 percent (Greve, 1972).

Victim Surveys 1984

No victim surveys have been conducted in Zürich since Clinard's in 1973 (one is planned for 1987/88). But two such studies have been made in other parts of Switzerland.

One was conducted in the French-speaking region of Switzerland (Killias, 1985). About one-fifth of the Swiss population live in this region. The study was made in 1984 by means of telephone interviews with 3,000 persons, but was supplemented with personal interviews and mail questionnaires to a sub-sample. The method used involves several interesting experimental components which, at the same time, make it problematic and risky to compare it with other studies. However, comparisons using simple theft are possible.

In 1984 almost 9 percent of the inhabitants in the French-speaking region of Switzerland claimed that during the previous year they had been victims of simple theft, that is, thefts excluding break-ins and thefts of means of transportation. In an opinion poll by AIM in Denmark in the autumn of 1984, 3 percent claimed to have been subjected to thefts other than burglary or theft of vehicles over the preceding half-year (Andersen, 1985). Thus in Switzerland, the question covered a period twice as long, but the resulting rate is three times as great.

The frequency of burglaries in these studies is not directly comparable, but there does not seem to be any difference of note. Over a period of one year, 1 percent of the population in the French-speaking region of Switzerland had been burgled in their homes. The risk in 1977 of such a crime in Denmark was 0.6 percent. According to the Danish crime statistics, the risk rose by 75 percent from 1977 to 1984, which would mean a total risk in 1984 identical to that in the French-speaking part of Switzerland, i.e. 1 percent. Differences may exist, however, in the definition of 'home' or 'residence' and variations in the specific formulation of the questions would also lead to dissimilar results.

The other victim survey in Switzerland since 1973 was conducted in the Canton of Uri, which is one of the three oldest cantons in Switzerland. It is geographically situated in the German-speaking part of the country and is inhabited by an overwhelmingly Catholic population. It lies in a primarily agricultural region. The largest city in the Canton is Altdorf, with some 10,000 inhabitants. The entire canton had a population of 33,000 in 1984.

The victim survey in Uri was also conducted in 1984 (Stadler, 1986). It consisted of mail questionnaires and responses from a representative sample of 265 of Uri's 20 years old and older population. The question on thefts and vandalism was in essence identical to the one that has been used several times in national studies in Denmark, most recently in 1982. The lower age limit in the Danish study is 15 years. This difference in age limits for the selected interviewees, however, probably does not affect the overall victimization rates very much.

Fig. 18 shows how large a proportion of the population in the Canton of Uri and in Denmark claimed to have been the victims of thefts in 1984 and 1982, respectively. In the Canton of Uri, 17 percent made this claim compared to 15 percent for the whole of Denmark. The most reasonable procedure is to compare the theft rates in Uri with the theft rates among the rural population 20 years old or older in Denmark. This rate was only half as great as the rate in Uri.

Could this be due to the fact that thefts were more concentrated among single victims in Denmark? This has been shown not to be the case. In the Canton of Uri, there were 29 thefts per 100 inhabitants, or an average of 1.71 per victim. For Denmark as a

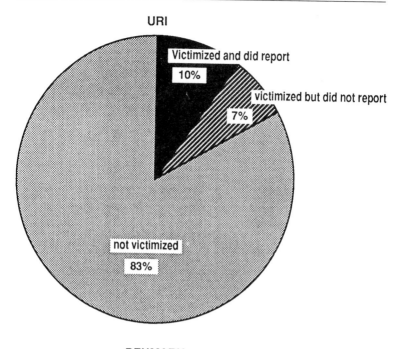

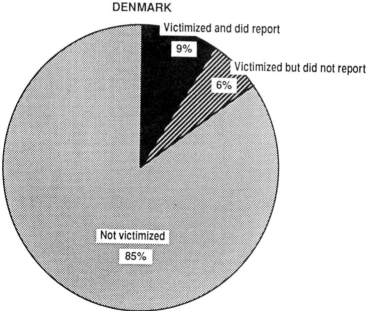

Fig. 18. Victims of theft, Canton Uri 1984 and Denmark 1982

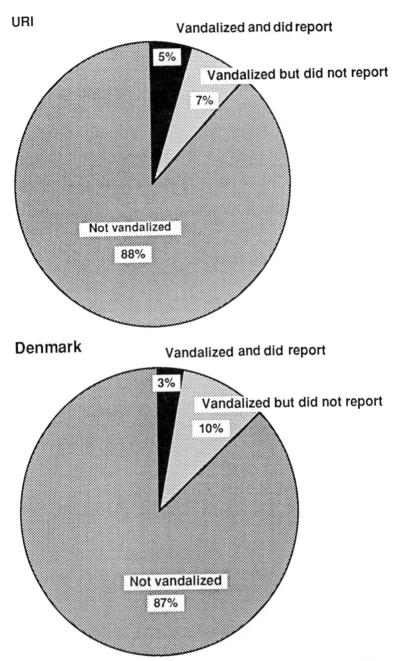

Fig. 19. Victims of vandalism, Canton Uri 1984 and Denmark 1982

whole, there were 25 thefts per 100 inhabitants, or an average of 1.65 per victim.

The similarity for vandalism is also striking. It is shown in Fig. 19 that 12 percent had been vandalized in Uri in 1984 compared to 13 percent in Denmark as a whole in 1982.

Nor is there any important difference in the rates at which the victims had been subjected to vandalism. The number of acts of vandalism in the Canton of Uri per 100 inhabitants was 25. For Denmark, it was 22.

In both the Uri and the Danish studies interviewees were asked whether they had reported the crimes to the police. In Uri, 59 percent of the theft victims had gone to the police, and in Denmark, 60 percent. In total, 38 percent of the thefts in Uri had been reported compared to 44 percent in Denmark. Of the victims of vandalism 42 percent in Uri and 23 percent in Denmark reported the crimes to the police. In total, 24 percent of the cases of vandalism in Uri and 14 percent of those in Denmark were reported. Thus, in Denmark there is a statistically significantly lower tendency to report vandalism to the police.

In the light of the totals of theft and vandalism and the prevailing tendencies to report crimes in Denmark and in Uri, it could be

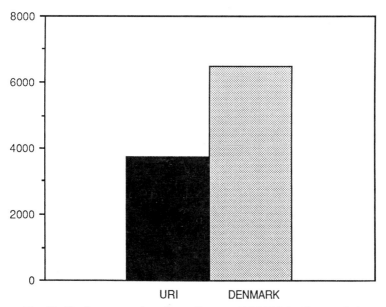

Fig. 20. Thefts reported to the police per 100,000 inhabitants 1983

expected that police figures on registered thefts would be on about the same level. As regards vandalism, we could expect a somewhat higher level of registered acts in the Canton of Uri. But neither of these expectations materializes (see Figs. 20 and 21). Local statistics show that the Uri police registered 3,733 thefts per 100,000 inhabitants in 1983 (*Rechenschaftsbericht*, 1984). In Denmark, the corresponding figure was 74 percent higher, that is, 6502. In Uri, 271 cases of vandalism per 100,000 inhabitants were registered in 1983, and in Denmark 78 percent more, that is, 483. This indicates—as was true in 1973—that the Swiss police are to an unusual degree still keeping crime figures down by bypassing many crime reports either by not recording them on paper or by not counting them in their compilations of crime figures.

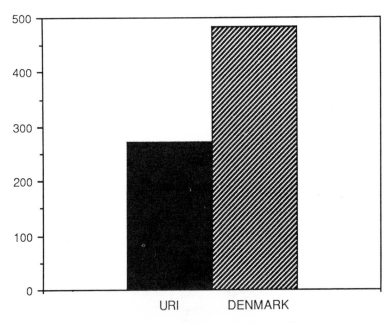

Fig. 21. Cases of vandalism reported to the police per 100,000 inhabitants 1983

This is also confirmed by the fact that several victims in the Uri study stated that the police refused to register some complaints such as those relating to thefts from automobiles. A follow-up of the Uri study showed that almost one-third of the matters claimed by the interviewed victims to have been reported to the cantonal police could not later be found in the police register. Similar studies show that in Denmark this rate was only half as large.

Conclusion

In conclusion, these attempts at estimating the total volume of theft, vandalism, and violence indicate that there are no pronounced or remarkable differences between Switzerland and Denmark, either today or 10–15 years ago. What is pronounced and remarkable, however, is that the Swiss police have a certain tendency to omit traditional criminality from their statistics.

7

Control Downwards and Upwards in Society

A country should not be judged on the basis of its level of crime alone, but also on its manner of controlling crime. A country may be able to reduce its level of shoplifting by chopping off the hands of thieves, but it must be asked whether this type of control is not more unacceptable than the act it is aimed at holding in check.

The apparatus for controlling crime has two sides, one punitive and one non-punitive. In this chapter, we will deal mainly with non-punitive control, that is, the general efforts of a society to prevent and react to crime within the labor market and social and educational spheres. Beyond what is said elsewhere in this book concerning punitive reactions, we will simply state here that the Swiss penal system resembles the Danish one in many important aspects.

The non-punitive side of crime control in its turn has two sides: the control of groups that are seen as menacing, and the control of groups that are not seen as menacing, especially of the controllers themselves. In class societies such as those in Switzerland and Denmark this is essentially translated into control over the worst-off groups in society, on the one hand, and the control that the best situated groups in society impose on themselves, on the other. In more concrete terms, it is a question of how you try to prevent traditional crimes such as thefts, vandalism and the like, crimes typical of young persons, unskilled workers, or the unemployed in the cities; and how you try to prevent corporate crime such as real estate speculation, tax fraud, pollution of the environment, abuse of power and the like, which are forms of behavior typical of economically strong and powerful groups in the society.

Here we shall try to show that the Swiss society tries to control and prevent crime in ways that are remarkably different from those used in Denmark. The control and the supervision are unusually strict when aimed at the unfortunate, but quite relaxed when aimed at the well-to-do. First, we will look at the control of the weak, or those groups among the weak who are traditionally viewed as 'the dangerous underclass': young unskilled or unemployed men in the cities.

Control of the Bottom Echelons of Society

It has been remarked that Switzerland begins at the middle class. This connotes that the working class is relatively small in Switzerland especially the unskilled segment (see Chapter 8 for further details), but also that the working class has a particular composition and position in the Swiss society. The working class largely consists of non-Swiss: foreign nationals without Swiss citizenship. Inversely, one could say that a large portion of the foreigners living in Switzerland without Swiss citizenship have the status of and are employed as laborers. About 5 million of the inhabitants of Switzerland have Swiss citizenship. There are an additional one million inhabitants without Swiss citizenship, that is, 16–17 percent of the total population are foreigners.

Just a few figures are needed to show the substantial coincidence of foreigners as a group, on the one hand, and the (unskilled) working class on the other—especially the young, city-dwelling and laboring section of it. Among the native Swiss, 45 percent belong to the group of persons gainfully employed, but among the foreigners, this figure is 61 percent. Of those gainfully employed, 34 percent of the native Swiss are workers, but 76 percent of the foreigners. While 13 percent of the Swiss are self-employed, only 2 percent of the foreigners are. The tendency you find in Denmark and other countries for many foreign workers to be employed within the service industries and as managers of small businesses and shops, kiosks, and so on, is not found in Switzerland. The reason for this is a basic reluctance to give foreign workers licenses to conduct these types of businesses. Inversely again, a clear majority of the working class consists of foreigners, not least of all among the unskilled workers. The precise percentages vary slightly with how the working class is delimited.

Statistics support the statement that foreigners in Switzerland are mainly young, unskilled men in the cities, and conversely, that young, unskilled men in Switzerland are mainly foreigners.

The status of Switzerland as an importer of labor power is a relatively new one. Before industrialization, the situation was the opposite. As a result of overpopulation in relation to jobs available and the omnipresent poverty, many Swiss emigrated and/or took work in other countries, the best known example being service as mercenary soldiers. In the 1700s, Switzerland lost one-fifth of its population through emigration. But as a consequence of the enormous road and railway construction, this trend was reversed at the beginning of the present century, and up to the First World War, the number of foreigners in Switzerland increased sharply. At first, it was mainly Germans and French who came to Switzerland for work, but later the Italians dominated. Around the time of the First World War, the level of foreigners was similar to that of today, 16–17 percent. During the worldwide crisis in the 1930s, most foreigners were sent out of Switzerland again, a regulation of the labor force so effective that, in contrast to what happened in most other countries, the level of unemployment was kept quite low (6–7 percent at its peak). The percentage of foreigners in the Swiss population fell to 5 percent during this period.

One of the main reasons for the exceptionally high standard of living in Switzerland today is its successful policy of neutrality during the Second World War. The unscathed production apparatus left the country in a good position concerning supplies and well able to compete when the war was over. Demand rose so sharply that a shortage of labor quickly arose. Therefore, the regulations on employing foreign labor were eased and the ranks of foreigners began to swell again, and did so until the early 1970s. Since 1960, the numbers of Spaniards, Yugoslavians, and Turks among the inflow of foreigners have especially increased.

Over the past 20 years, the trends in unemployment in Switzerland and in Denmark have been remarkably similar. But there is one crucial difference: the yardstick for the Danish curve is *percentage* and for the Swiss curve, *per thousand*. If these curves were taken at face value, unemployment would be almost nonexistent in Switzerland. Especially striking are the only slight increases since the middle of the 1970s.

In the light of the unemployment curves, it would seem that Switzerland has managed completely to elude the economic setbacks that have hit other countries so hard. The truth is, however, that the Swiss society has once again, as was done in the 1930s, used foreigners as *buffers against market trends*. In fact, the economic setback in the 1970s was greater in Switzerland than in Denmark. Whereas a large part of Denmark's unemployment problem in recent years has stemmed from more people seeking jobs rather than from there being less jobs to be sought, Switzerland lost no less than 10 percent of its jobs over the two-year period from 1974 to 1976. This translates into 340,000 jobs. Unemployment rose, however, by only 13,000. The problem was 'solved' by sending several hundred thousand foreign workers out of the country as well as by excluding more women from the labor market. If Switzerland had 'behaved' towards its foreign workers in the same way as Denmark did during this period, it would have been faced with a still greater unemployment problem than Denmark.

This reflects not only a national selfishness, but also a particular approach towards work and unemployment in Switzerland. To a unique extent work and diligence are perceived as the road to success, both for the individual and for the country as a whole. The Calvinistic ideology, with its emphasis on work, diligence, and thriftiness, has had a strong grasp on the Swiss population, and has remained more intact and unchallenged here than in most other western societies. It was Calvin himself (in the French region) together with Zwingli (in the German region) who brought the reformation to Switzerland. Illustrative of this attitude is an article from February 1986 in one of the country's largest newspapers. The article was on 'drugs', dependence-producing substances, but not the usual ones such as tobacco, alcohol, narcotics, or coffee. The dependence-producing substance in this article was *work*. Eight pages were spent on interviews with persons sharing the same problem, workaholism, under the title, *Arbeit als droge*.

The Calvinistic outlook is reflected in a strong anxiety about unemployment. Even changes per thousands in the level of unemployment give rise to long newspaper articles and lively debate. During some months in 1985, for example, anxiety and attention was focussed on how unemployment topped 'the critical level': 1 percent. Unemployment for a Swiss is seen as a personal defeat and an occasion of great shame. An interview survey from 1986 showed that over half the Swiss population regarded unemployment as self-induced. Half also considered unemployed persons as social outsiders on a par with rockers, hippies, and the like, and drug problems and criminality as consequences of unemployment. In February 1986, one newspaper interviewed six unemployed persons. Characteristically, no photographs of them were shown. A back view of one of the interviewees was shown, and six small shots of the interviewees' hands.

The intense shame associated with being unemployed in Switzerland implies that the unemployment statistics are a particularly bad gauge of the dimensions of the problem. Many people do not have unemployment insurance, and many others are loath to register officially as unemployed, which is a prerequisite to appearing in the statistics. This gives us special reason to believe that hidden unemployment among women is widespread.

Another consequence is that the burden of unemployment will fall on the most powerless more so than elsewhere in the society. A Swiss would be reluctant to banish another Swiss to the ranks of the unemployed except as a last resort. Therefore, it must be the foreigners who bear the brunt, and so as not to impose an economic burden on others or to cause problems when they become unemployed, e.g. by committing crimes, they must leave the country.

The administrative and political superstructure of this general outlook and the particular view of the rights and duties of foreigners in the Swiss society are formally expressed in the control and legal provisions to the effect that the rights of foreigners to be in Switzerland are narrowly linked to the desirability of their labor power. Foreigners may gain the right to be in Switzerland when there is work for them and when they are suited for this work. But if there is no work or if they are not suited for it—or do not behave themselves to their neighbors', employers', or others' liking—then there is no place for them.

Moreover, this massive program to discipline foreigners is extensively fragmented so that a labyrinth of work and residence permits creates a situation in which foreigners as a group do not see themselves as having common interests. The basic forms for these permits are given below:

Border commuters (*Grenzgängern*) are those foreign citizens who have got permission to work in Switzerland but not to live there. They are allowed to commute back and forth every day. The permit is usually limited in time, and always linked to a certain job at a particular workplace. If the worker loses this specific job, the permit is lost as well.

Seasonal workers (*Saisonniers*/A-permit) are foreign citizens who have got permission to work in Switzerland for 9 months at a time. After these nine months are over, they must leave Switzerland for at least three months, before seeking to renew the 9-months permit. This permit is also linked to a particular job. It is permitted for these workers to live in Switzerland during the nine months, but they are not allowed to bring their families with them.

The third level in the hierarchy consists of those foreign citizens who receive a *work and residence permit for one year* (*Jahrenaufenhaltsbewillung*/B-permit). It is more than a formality to renew this permit each year. Renewal depends upon whether the worker has work as well as a good reputation. Permission again is linked to a particular job.

A *full work and residence permit* (*Niederlassungsbewillung*/C-permit) is also limited in time, but as long as the worker has a job, the renewal after three years and then after five years is normally just a formality. Workers with *Niederlassungsbewillung* permits for over 10 years can even renew them if they are temporarily out of work at the time of seeking a renewal, and the permit will not be withdrawn if the worker is temporarily unemployed during the duration of the permit. Foreigners living and working in Switzerland with this type of permit have on the average been there for more than 10 years. A work and residence permit is typically subject to the condition of a job-freeze period (*Sperrfrist*). Until 1968, workers on these permits were not allowed to change jobs on their own initiative during the first five years. This 'job-freeze' period is now one year. In this way, foreigners in the country function as a stable labor force.

The final level naturally is *Swiss citizenship*, which is extremely difficult to achieve. Over the past 30 years, the average number of naturalized Swiss has been about 3,000 yearly, which is not very much in a country with one million foreigners. But this level has been about twice as high over the last 10 years. Requirements for attaining Swiss citizenship include a long-term domicile there, permanent work, and an irreproachable reputation among neighbors, employers, and possibly children's teachers, and so on, but also the payment of a considerable sum of money. This amount fluctuates among the municipalities and cantons, but $5,000 is not unusual.

During economic crises, foreigners at the bottom of the hierarchy sketched above are sent out of the country, while at the same time conditions for entering higher levels in the hierarchy are tightened up.

The labor-market policy applied to foreign workers is aimed not only at regulating unemployment, but also at a structural reorganization of the Swiss labor market. The objective is to ensure that the Swiss first of all get the newly created jobs in the growth industries, while it is first of all foreign workers who lose the jobs eliminated in dying industries. An example of this is that 18 percent of the employees in the watch industry lost their jobs from 1975 to 1980—this represented 33 percent of the foreigners working there and only 10 percent of the Swiss. Inversely, 16 percent more employees were hired by the banking industry, representing only 4 percent more foreigners but 18 percent more Swiss. Within the health service sector, 17 percent new positions were added, but this hides the fact that Swiss employees increased by 28 percent while the number of foreigners dropped by 7 percent.

In such an immigration policy, *criminality* functions as an *ideological varnish*. The risk of crime—not least the risk of drug crimes—has been used to legitimate the policy adopted and the measures implemented. The strict control and supervision of foreigners—the Swiss society's working class—is motivated and substantiated by the apprehension that without this control, enormous problems would emerge with thieving, drug-dealing, and other crimes and social problems. According to the Swiss, the immigration policy is an effective and necessary criminal policy and crime prevention measure. The logic of the ideological varnish for the immigration policy is summarized in the following doctrines or propositions:

1) Unemployed people turn to crime.
2) Crime is contagious, and spreads like rings in water to contribute to the dissolution of society.
3) Foreigners are more criminal than the Swiss, and
4) Unemployed foreigners are especially criminal.

Obviously belief in these statements could easily lead to the conviction that as few foreigners as possible ought to be allowed to reside in Switzerland, that those who are already there should be subjected to as much control, supervison, and discipline as possible, and that, above all, foreigners should not be allowed to stay if they become unemployed.

In its most rabid form, this logic and its conclusions encourage the belief that the foreigners now in Switzerland should be sent home, and that no additional foreigners should receive work and residence permits. A referendum was called in the middle of the 1960s with just this type of demand, the *Ueberfremdung* initiative.

Later a political party the *Nationale Aktion gegen Ueberfremdung von Volk und Heimat*, was hatched from this initiative. Party voters in parliamentary elections have endorsed this far-right party as follows:

1967	0.6 percent
1971	7.2 percent
1975	5.5 percent
1979	1.9 percent
1983	3.5 percent

During my stay in Switzerland in February 1986, an intense discussion about refugees was under way. Characteristically, it became a question of how many more refugees, if any, should be admitted and what should be done with them—linked, on the one hand, to the risk of rising unemployment, and on the other, to the risk of rising criminality.

Discontent was high about the fact that many of the refugees did not have jobs. It was also asserted that many refugees traded in heroin, especially after it was revealed that one group of Tamils from Sri Lanka took part in illegal drug operations. The ensuing discussion led to the passing of a new law making it both easier and quicker to expel refugees from the country.

Perhaps it should also be mentioned that this tough immigration and refugee policy meets and has met with strong opposition from many quarters in Switzerland. The church in particular has reacted forcefully against the sharper stance being taken against refugees. The church has proclaimed it illegal to remove refugees from church grounds by force. *Ueberfremdung* initiatives—referendums on the presence of foreigners in Switzerland—have had unusually high voter turn-outs, and the majority opinion among the population has not been in favor of the most rabid immigration and refugee policies. One of the initiatives called for the expulsion of 70 percent of the foreign population. About 45 percent voted for this proposal, 55 percent against.

An illustration of the special supervision and suspicion to which foreigners are subjected by the police is the official crime statistics for the Canton of Uri for 1984. These show that 82 arrests were made on the suspicion of crime. Of the 82 who were arrested, 57 were foreigners. Of the 102 crimes that were cleared up on the basis of these arrests only two were committed by foreigners (Stadler, 1986).

Export of Crime Problems

The Swiss crime statistics do not suggest that crimes such as thefts and violence are notably more often committed by foreigners than by native Swiss. However, it cannot be excluded that foreigners *would become* criminal to a greater extent or that criminality thereby *would become* greater in Switzerland if foreigners were allowed to stay there when unemployed. The harsh rejection that confronts unemployed persons in Switzerland and their crippled financial situation might well lead to more criminality—for foreigners as well as for Swiss in the same situation. Therefore, perhaps the best way to characterize the control of the Swiss society over the working class and foreigners is as the export of (potential) crime problems. The problems are exported to Italy, Spain, Yugoslavia, and the other countries from which the foreign workers originate. In their home countries, the expelled find themselves in an even worse situation, with an even worse financial position, and an even slimmer chance of finding work than they would have had in Switzerland. It seems reasonable then to assume that the risk of criminality is greater after the 'export' of these persons than it would have been had they been allowed to remain.

Switzerland can also be said to export its problems in yet another way. There are very few slum areas in Swiss cities, but analyses of Switzerland's economic transactions abroad have shown that it perhaps more than any other country is responsible for the existence of slums outside of its own borders (Ziegler, 1977). The paradox lies in the fact that many of the persons exported are compelled to live in slum areas when sent back to their home country, areas financed by Swiss capital and on which Switzerland has earned and earns large sums of money. Living in these areas could hardly have a mitigating effect on the potential problems that make up the backdrop to these people's expulsion from Switzerland.

, A specific export of crime and criminals from Switzerland is found in the deportations of many foreigners arrested for crime. There *are* situations in which foreigners who are arrested have not been deported immediately or even after serving sentences, but deportation is used for a wider range of crimes and against a broader group of foreigners than is the case in Denmark. In February 1986, a Sicilian who had lived in Switzerland for 24 years was deported. His crime was attempting to extort money from a shopkeeper by demanding protection money. It was done very amateurishly and stopped in the attempt phase. He was alone in this extortion attempt and was trying to set right a desperate economic situation. He was sentenced to 27 months in prison to be followed by 15 years' expulsion.

Deportations may be decided administratively or in a court of law. All criminal matters involving foreigners, whether they are domiciled or mere tourists in Switzerland, are passed on to the Aliens Police. The Aliens Police have the administrative powers to deport these foreigners. There is no appeal. Deportations may range from 1 to 15 years, or for life.

Another consequence of its policies for other countries is the fact that, despite its position as the most affluent country in Western Europe, Switzerland ranks very low on the list for assistance to developing countries. Switzerland's foreign aid amounts to a mere 0.25 percent of its GNP (1982). This seems strange for a country which has a tradition of humanitarian and relief work and which houses the headquarters of the International Red Cross and Terre des Hommes. It seems to rest on the notion that Switzerland only has a limited responsibility to Third World countries, because it has not been a warring nation and even more so because it has never been a colonial power. In relative terms, Denmark appropriated three times more than Switzerland did in 1982 for such aid, and Austria twice as much.

Control at the Top of Society

Now we have come closer to the other side of the control question, namely, controlling the controllers. One issue here is to what degree and how should corporate crime, such as real estate speculation, pollution, and the like, be prevented and controlled. To his great credit, Clinard included corporate crime in his analysis of the Swiss crime situation. He concluded that in contrast to traditional criminality, corporate crime seems to be prevalent in Switzerland. An updated review of the situation in 1986 supports this conclusion.

First, the Swiss society allows and provides more opportunity for economic exploitation and profiteering than is the case in Denmark. The best known example of this is the possibility of maintaining a secret bank account where one's economic transactions are concealed. Banks have the power to decide whether or not to offer a customer a secret account, a so-called number account, where the customer's name is known only to the director of the bank, and where all transactions take place via a number and a *code*. Correspondence between the bank and the client is often indirect, e.g. via a senior bank clerk's private address. Normally, a deposit of a significant amount of money is a precondition for such number accounts. Current law forbids banks to receive money that they suspect to be the fruit of illegal transactions, but in practice it is easy to 'launder' money. Interest rates are low, so that the banks can earn a lot of money on the deposited funds. Customers can also get the bank to put their money to work. An American business executive, for example, can order the bank to buy shares in his own company on the New York Stock Exchange. The value of the shares is thus forced up, and he can sell them again when the prices are higher.

The fact of bank secrecy in Switzerland has both a general and a more special and concrete explanation. The powerful grip that Calvinism has had on the Swiss society has already been mentioned. Bank secrecy in general can be seen as a manifestation of this philosophy. An individual's work capacity, diligence, and thriftiness are highly valued, and a distinctive feature of this philosophy is that one must be discreet about success. External symbols of success should not be conspicuous. The result of one's efforts, money, is to be put in the bank, where full discretion is demanded— and given. More particularly, the historical background to bank secrecy stems from Switzerland's role as a refuge for people fleeing from persecution in their own country. The identities of refugees were protected through bank secrecy. This occurred most frequently after the Nazis came to power in Germany. It was during this period that bank secrecy became entrenched by statute in the Swiss society. Many people fled from National Socialistic Germany, from which it was strictly forbidden to removal capital.

The code of bank secrecy has in principle been curbed somewhat in recent years, primarily in the wake of a great scandal in 1977 starring one of Switzerland's three largest banks, *Crédit Suisse Bank*. Over a long period prior to the exposure, Italian lire had been flowing into this bank's branch in Chiasso from more or less legal activities in Italy. At one point, the Italian lire fell sharply in relation to the Swiss franc. To avoid large losses on these holdings of lire, the government introduced an annual negative 10 percent interest. In reaction, the Chiasso branch office, either directly without entering the money in any account or via secret accounts, began loaning the lire to a finance house in Liechtenstein, which in turn bought shares in Italian companies—the result of which was a substantial profit for the bank and the owners of the lire. The amount involved was more than one billion US$. The bank was fined 30 million US$ for its transactions. After this scandal, the government tightened the reins, making it more difficult for foreigners to deposit their money—especially black market money—in number accounts, as well as more difficult to open new banks. However, not much seems to have changed in practice. Bypassing any extensive formalities, I was readily offered the chance to open a number account in February 1986 at a Zürich bank, on the condition of a deposit of 100,000 Danish crowns, i.e. about 15,000 US$, which were to be forwarded later, identified only by the account number. (*However, the process stopped here. A Danish criminologist does not earn or possess the cash necessary to play any real part in this game!*)

In recent years and especially in the Italian-speaking Canton of Tessin, banks have been suspected of basing their operations on Italian Mafia money derived from drug-trafficking, among other things. It is clear that the banks in this area have grown much faster and more new banks have been opened than is the case in other areas. The culmination to date of this debate was reached when one of the leading figures in a big Mafia trial in Palermo died in a hospital in Tessin. As he was suffering from cancer, he was not detained pending trial. His death raised the question of why he went to Tessin. Over the preceding months, a growing number of known Mafiosi from Italy had been seen in Zürich and other financial centers.

Second, the Swiss society does not just provide a very favorable setting for legal as well as illegal profiteering. Illegal profiteering *is* in fact also widespread. Apart from the undoubtedly enormous dark figure, there is a constant stream of trials being conducted involving colossal sums of money. In February 1986, investigations began in a case against a financial house whose owners had by then fled to the USA. Within a rather short period of time, they had tricked investors out of about 150 million US$. This amount is about the same as the total loss in Denmark from all thefts in one year.

The cantonal police in Zürich have a special unit for dealing with corporate or business crime. From this unit's annual report, the number of cases investigated as well as the dimensions of the illegal gains can be seen:

Year	Number of cases	Illegal gains in US$ (millions)
1974	104	102
1975	105	112
1976	124	202
1977	120	168
1978	141	127
1979	150	96
1980	154	103
1981	172	91
1982	183	141
1983	154	150

The Canton of Zürich is inhabited by about 1 million people. Between one-fourth and one-fifth of the cases are bankruptcy cases, involving an average total of unpaid debts of over 15 million US$ each year. The official figure for all untaxed wealth in the form of property in Switzerland is not less than 70 billion US$.

In his empirical criminological study from the 1930s, Hacker concluded that business crime in Switzerland was very extensive in relation to its neighboring countries. He interpreted this as an indication of the pinnacle of civilization achieved in Switzerland: 'Jo hoher die Zivilisation eines Landes, umso mehr Betrugsdelikte' (Hacker, 1939): The more developed the civilization in a country, the more crimes of fraud.

Third, neither have the necessary resources been set aside for combating business crime, nor has the necessary structure been built.

It is the rare canton that, like Zürich, has a special police unit for business crime. There is no special unit, for example, in the neighboring Canton of Zug, despite the fact that many of the bigger cases have originated there. The explanation for this is not to be found in any lack of population or economic resources. Zug is the richest canton in Switzerland. The average wage in the Canton of Zug corresponds to about 35,000 US$, which is double the average for the whole of Switzerland (1984). Add to this a taxation rate of only half the normal. One percent of the Swiss population lives here, but the canton is known for its 'enterprising' atmosphere and it is the home of 7 percent of the companies of Switzerland, above all several multi-national corporations.

There is no *federal* body with the resources or powers to take over. Control is the responsibility of the individual *cantons*. Much of the corporate criminality, however, crosses cantonal lines and/ or moves between the cantons. In such cases, it is up to the cantons involved in the transactions to indicate counter-measures jointly. The prevailing approach is one of resignation. It is generally accepted that with the resources currently available and with the present control structure, there is not much to fight the problem with. Nor is there any hope of succeeding in the individual cases, if the offender possesses even the slightest degree of finesse.

The Overall Picture of Control

An overall and critical evaluation of the means of control and supervision generally used for preventing crime in Switzerland leads us to three conclusions:

1) There is a remarkably and disproportionately vigorous control and supervision of persons holding the weakest position in society and of their potential criminality.
2) There is a remarkably and disproportionately feeble control and supervision of those holding the strongest positions and of their potential criminality.
3) Combining these two statements illustrates that the intensity of the control apparatus in a rather extreme way operates inversely to the volume of and damage caused by the existing crime problems.

Presumably, the control structure has the two following effects:
First, to a considerable degree, Switzerland exports 'traditional' crime problems, such as violence, theft, and drugs to other countries.

Second, to a considerable degree, Switzerland promotes 'modern' criminality, such as business crimes.

If to these factors is added the notion put forward earlier that the 'traditional' crime problems in Switzerland are not less than those in Denmark, it becomes exceptionally difficult to maintain and understand the perception of Switzerland as a land of little crime.

8

Society's Control of Itself

In the concluding comments to his 1973 study, Clinard states that criminality in Switzerland was perhaps higher than he had first expected, but that, even so, it was remarkably low.

Re-analyzing the original material and following up the situation into the 1980s has revealed that criminality in Switzerland was indeed higher than could be expected. It is in fact so much higher that, seen from a *Danish* perspective, it could not be said to be unusually low. In the early 1970s the level of traditional crimes was *perhaps* lower than the Danish level, but not as low as, say, that of Norway or even neighboring Austria. In the early 1980s, the Swiss rates for theft, violence, and the like, were at least on a par with the Danish.

With this, the story could come to an end. A full stop could be set to this *methodological* story of defective collection of elementary data, with similar defects in systematism, self-analysis of one's own values, and a critical approach to and analysis of existing information. It would be a far from uncommon story within the field of criminology, especially where comparative studies are concerned.

But the story has, and also should have, a *theoretical* side. Clinard, as well as Adler, try to explain their low crime statements by emphasizing other unique aspects of the Swiss society. Some of these are of great interest, both theoretically and as a matter of principle. Two receive special attention:

1) the enhanced control over one's own life that can result from a relatively strong decentralization and involvement of the population in central decision-making processes, and the related
2) more rigorous informal social control among people that may result from low urbanization.

Furthermore, Clinard and Adler both stress a more traditional and strong moral formation, but this is an attempt at an explanation of a somewhat circular nature in that crime is implicitly used as an indicator of the degree of moral disassociation from criminal actions.

It is true that the political, administrative, and municipal structure in Switzerland differs from those in many other Western societies, including Denmark. In Switzerland, many political decisions are made at lower levels than is the case in Denmark. The population is drawn into the political decision-making process and into administration at various points and areas, which again is not the case in Denmark. There are no cities comparable in size to Copenhagen. At first glance, it would in the light of several criminological theories and ideas be reasonable to expect that this would act as a brake on traditional crimes, such as thefts, violence, and vandalism. It is generally assumed that much criminality is linked to powerlessness and/or a defective informal social control.

If this is so, why has this unique political, administrative, and municipal structure *not reduced* or slowed the criminality in Switzerland compared to Denmark and other Western countries? To answer this question, it is necessary to describe some of the features of the Swiss societal structure and historical background in more detail.

Urbanization

We can start off with the lack of big cities. Zürich is the largest city in Switzerland. But Zürich is not a 'million people city'. There is no city with over one million inhabitants in Switzerland—in contrast to the neighboring countries of France, Italy, Austria, and West Germany. At the last count, there were about 380,000 people living in Zürich proper, and about 700,000 when the surrounding suburbs are included. There are three partially related reasons for the fact that population peaks have been blunted in Switzerland's big cities compared to elsewhere, namely the country's cantonal structure, the special way in which industrialization has occurred, and the country's geographical setting and natural resources.

In earlier periods prior to the real industrialization, Switzerland had two large and dominant 'industries'—the *textile industry* centered in the German-speaking part of the country, and the *clock industry* centered in the French-speaking part. Switzerland was supreme in the clock market, and controlled a large part of the textile export in Europe as well. Overall, Switzerland was the 'industrial' center of Europe in the 1700s. During this period and far into the 1800s, the work performed in the clock and textile 'industries' had the character of cottage industries, where the farmers were at home part-time making watches or knitting clothes which they afterwards delivered to the nearest 'factory'. These 'factories' functioned more or less as warehouses or markets. The 'factories' were widely spread out in order to accommodate the farmers who had to travel long distances. Two other conditions prompted this decentralization. First, the lack of coal meant that people were extremely dependent on water power for their energy, and the natural water sources were also spread out and each endowed with only limited capacity. Second, *the guilds* played a decisive role when they located new operations in the countryside of many cantons in order to alleviate the poverty there. Their sole motivation, however, was not altruistic, but was at least as much due to their difficulty in approving of or accepting the textile princes and experts who had moved away from the Catholic parts of the country during the Reformation.

During Napoleon's short-lived, and in the long-run unsuccessful, attempt at establishing the Republic of Helvetia, all the power was concentrated in the towns, and the rural dwellers were brutally oppressed. This incited many rebellions among the farmers in the early 1800s. This was also a major reason why *the guilds* subsequently restricted the structure of the towns, and to such a degree, that industrialization in Switzerland can be seen as having made its first advances in the rural districts. This in turn resulted in the development of a very close bond between the small village and its (most important) local factory, whose owner often became a kind of quasi-mayor. In this way, industrial workers—more so than in other countries—lived for a long period of time in a narrow, paternalistic atmosphere characterized by strict social control and relatively close relationships between factory-owners and employees, a relationship that resembled the patriarchal family more than a traditional factory.

When the real industrialization came, it came very quickly, because only a limited construction of new factories was necessary. The existing ones were mechanized. If the technical side of industrialization came about very quickly—being 'only' a matter of introducing mechanical principles into already existing operations—the social side was unusually gradual, slow, and nearly imperceptible. It was the same people who continued to work at the same factories, typically on a part-time basis. The fact that the industrial development had its base in the rural communities, both for labor and geographical reasons, is also the explanation why the production of chocolate, which is based on the agricultural product milk, later grew into a strong and significant economic force in Switzerland. Another 'derivative' industry is the chemical industry, especially pharmaceuticals, in which Switzerland has taken a prominent lead over the years. This grew out of the textile industry with its skills and know-how about the dyeing of fabrics.

This special decentralized form of industralization in Switzerland with its agrarian roots is the main reason why the working class struggle in Switzerland has been less intense than in so many other countries. It is also the reason for the comparative lack of overcrowded slums in the larger cities so often found elsewhere in industrialized societies. Finally, it is the reason why the economic and class structure has evolved differently in Switzerland than elsewhere. First of all, it is characteristic that there have been fewer unskilled workers than in other countries. One contributory factor is Switzerland's complete lack of mineral resources, leading to insignificant heavy industry. The eventually superfluous Swiss farmers did not move into unskilled jobs, such as in the steel industry, but instead became skilled craftsmen, bank clerks, or the like. The usual urbanization stage was eliminated, and a leap was made directly from the agricultural society to the service society. Even when the industries were located in and near the towns and cities, they would usually hire a limited number of specialized workers and not a large number of unskilled ones because of their predominantly labor-intensive nature.

The specific class structure, the relatively peaceful labor market, and the relative absence of slums in the cities—three mutually related factors—are less pronounced today than previously, but they have left their permanent mark on Swiss society.

Water power and the absence of raw materials in the ground have been identified as natural conditions directly or indirectly helping to set an upper limit to the expansion of Swiss cities. A third contributory geographical factor is that Switzerland is landlocked. It is one of the few countries in Europe that does not border on the sea. The size of many other European cities has been determined precisely by their location by the sea and their function as a harbor town.

Finally, along with the lack of natural resources and the form that industrialization has taken, the country's unique cantonal structure has also helped to limit the size of the cities. The origin of Switzerland as a nation state goes back in time to 1291, when representatives of the three cantons of Uri, Schwyz, and Unterwald met and formed a confederacy. They agreed to defend each other against external enemies, and to assist one another in the face of internal unrest. It did not take long before several more cantons joined the confederacy. But even as late as the previous century, it was regarded more as a defense alliance than a nation state. Switzerland first became a nation state in 1848 after intense struggles, including a brief civil war. The federal constitution was adopted in 1848 and was amended again in 1874. This 1874 constitution is the one in force today. *Bundesverfassung der Schweizerischen Eidgenossenschaft* of 29 May 1874, begins by deeming Switzerland a federal union—*Confäderation Helvetica*— of 23 sovereign cantons. It clearly states that the goal of the union is to secure Switzerland's independence outwardly, to maintain peace and order internally, and to promote the common welfare. It emphasizes that the cantons are sovereign with regard to all areas for which this sovereignty is not explicitly limited by the constitution.

The sovereignty of the cantons is considerable and extensive— and was even more so earlier. This has meant that the country has developed 23 centers of power, instead of just one or two as in most other countries. Cantonal sovereignty has also meant that substantial disparities have developed among the cantons, which in their turn have inhibited inter-cantonal migration. The school systems, for example, often bear little resemblance to one another.

The school starting age differs from canton to canton, the length of compulsory school attendance varies by up to three years, the school year begins on different days, and the textbooks used are not the same. To change schools between cantons is almost like moving to a new school in another country. Other sources of great variation among the cantons are found in language and religion. Switzerland has three official languages—German, French, and Italian—but very few inhabitants are trilingual. The *ratoromanian* language should be added to this list, despite the fact that it is not an official language, and that by now it is only spoken by a relatively small group. About half of the population are Protestants and half Catholics. On combining the various dissimilarities, it quickly becomes clear that each canton has its own special profile that is rather different from that of all the others, inevitably making it troublesome to move back and forth across canton boundaries.

In that most of the cantons are rather small—with sometimes as few as 14,000 inhabitants—migration within the canton should not result in big cities. There is a total of one million inhabitants in the largest canton, Zürich.

In addition, the cantonal structure indirectly entails a far less centralized administration, with the accompanying ministries, administrative bodies, and so on, than is found in Denmark. Thus, there is not any one administrative center that would attract a concentration of people.

These factors together provide the key to understanding the striking fact that Switzerland is the only Western European country with more than five million inhabitants which has never had a city in the million-inhabitant range. It is a mistake, however, to equate this with an inconsequential urbanization, for instance, compared to Denmark.

First, the total population density of Switzerland is greater than that of Denmark. More people live in Switzerland, and the country's geographical area is smaller. In Switzerland, there are 154 inhabitants per square kilometer, which is 29 percent greater than in Denmark, which has 119 inhabitants per square kilometer. Add to this the fact that a much higher percentage of land is totally unavailable for building in Switzerland compared to Denmark. In fact, Switzerland is built up to practically full capacity, so that new dwellings can only be added by building onto existing houses. The Swiss urban planners stress the fact that Switzerland is overpopulated. Its maximum development is reflected in part in the extremely high rents and mortgages.

Second, it is 'only' a million-inhabitant city that is lacking in the Swiss city structure. The absence of such a city does not mean that there are no big cities in Switzerland. If we compare the number of cities with more than 100,000 inhabitants in Switzerland and in Denmark, we get the following picture (the figures include suburbs):

SWITZERLAND		DENMARK	
Zürich	708,400	Copenhagen	1,381,800
Basel	367,800	Århus	181,830
Geneva	324,900	Odense	136,646
Bern	282,400	Ålborg	114,302
Lausanne	227,300		
Lucerne	156,800		
Wintherthur	106,400		

Switzerland has seven cities with more than 100,000 inhabitants and Denmark four. The four next largest Swiss cities are also clearly larger than Denmark's next largest city. One-third of the total population in both countries live in cities with more than 100,000 inhabitants.

Third, when one considers the historical development of Swiss cities, it is important to consider not only the degree of urbanization of the most urbanized areas, but also that of the least urbanized areas. History shows that there has been some type of *inverse urbanization* in Switzerland, with the rural districts acquiring an urban character before, but especially during, industrialization. The typically urban structure of economic activity and the accompanying life style is thus characteristic of much smaller Swiss urban communities than could be found in Denmark. This is presumably the main reason why we find a level of theft and vandalism in the Canton of Uri, despite its small town character, that is comparable with that found in all of Denmark (see Chapter 6).

Fourth, the interesting thing in this context is more the living conditions and life style that characterize the cities than their size. The claim that there is more crime in big cities than in small towns is based on the assumption that the informal social control declines as the size of the city increases. However, this is not a natural law, as is shown by the example of Japan. Towns of the same size can have very disparate levels of crime, especially in different countries. This means that the character and range of the informal social control should be measured by concrete means whenever possible, and not only extrapolated from population density. One expression of a strong informal social control is by definition the readiness to intervene in situations where something undesirable is or has occurred. In the comparative victim surveys conducted in 1973 in Zürich and Stuttgart, a question was asked about readiness to intervene—at least by calling the police—if one witnessed a crime being committed (Stephan 1982). Less than half of those asked in Zürich said they would intervene, and interveners were fewer in Zürich than in Stuttgart.

In a more nuanced and historical perspective than the absence of a million-inhabitant city would provide, it is reasonable to conclude that if the very low degree of urbanization in Switzerland has not resulted in a very low criminality, it is simply because the characterization of Switzerland as especially under-urbanized is wrong.

Decentralization

The informal power over *other persons'* lives and existence does not seem to be particularly different in Switzerland than elsewhere, but what about the formal and real power over *one's own* existence? Has the unusual political and administrative structure in Switzerland reduced the powerlessness and ensuing alienation, compared to other Western nations like Denmark? It is easy to envisage such effects in the light of Switzerland's advanced system of direct democracy, the decentralization of many political decisions, and the frequent use of lay persons and non-professionals in both administration and politics. To answer the question, let us look at the basic features of the administrative and political structures in Switzerland.

There are two parliaments on the federal level—the *Nationalrat* with 200 members and the *Ständerat* with 46. All Swiss citizens 20 years old and older are eligible to vote in elections to these legislative bodies (some cantons have a voting age of 18 years). The *Nationalrat* is elected through proportional voting. There is no required minimum percentage of votes before a party may enter the Parliament. The Ständerat is elected through majority voting, with two members from each of the 23 cantons. Traditionally, this has meant that the Ständerat has been the more conservative body, owing to the relatively strong representation of the more rural cantons. The two chambers are on complete parity with one another, and no law can be passed without being approved by a majority in both. Normally, the two chambers consider the proposed laws separately, but at times they merge to work on specific issues in the *Bundesversamlung*. They merge, for instance, when a new *Bundesrat*, or government is to be elected.

There are seven permanent members in the government and it is traditionally a coalition government. After each election over the past 20 years, the government has been formed according to 'the golden rule', that is, not according to the voting results, but rather the principle of cooperation: two Social Democrats, two Liberals, two Christian Democrats, and one from the Agrarian Party. The only variation has been in the background of the seventh member of government. The seven Ministers are elected for four years and cannot be deposed during this period, just as the government on its part is not empowered to dissolve the Parliaments.

The government chooses one of its members to act as chairman presiding over the conduct of its proceedings. It is customary to select the person with the most seniority. The President, as this chairman is called, is designated for one year only and cannot be chosen for a new term until all the other members of the government have served as President. The post of President is a relatively insignificant one and without any independent powers.

Despite their very disparate interests, the representatives in the government are expected to conduct themselves as members of a unified collective at all times. It arouses disapprobation if a member outwardly expresses disagreement with a government decision.

When a bill has been drafted, usually by a commission appointed by one of the chambers, it must be submitted to a hearing by those interest groups who will be affected before it can be brought up in Parliament. All 23 cantons must be heard on the issues involved. It it is not uncommon for this round of hearings to take several years.

Referendums occupy a central position in the legislative process on the federal level. There are three kinds of referendum. First, there are *initiatives*. If their signatures are collected within a period of 18 months, 100,000 eligible voters can thereby demand that the constitution be amended if a simple majority in a referendum so requires. Initiatives on the federal level may only propose amendments to the constitution, which is the reason for the rather heterogeneous collection of articles that makes up the Swiss constitution. For example, there is an article in the constitution prohibiting the production and sale of absinth, a law that resulted from just this type of initiative.

The second type of referendum is the *mandatory referendum*. Before parliamentary decisions on amendments to the constitution take effect they must be approved in this type of referendum. A simple majority is required for a positive outcome in such referendums, as well as a simple majority in more than half of the cantons.

The third type is the *advisory referendum*. Through these, laws that are not part of the constitution—such as tax laws—can be submitted to the people if 50,000 eligible voters sign a petition declaring that they so desire, within 90 days after the passing of the law by Parliament. These referendums are decided by a simple majority.

The federal legislative structure is more or less reproduced on the cantonal level. The most significant difference is that on the cantonal level there is a one-chamber system and public initiatives may concern matters other than changes of the constitution. Every canton has its own constitution, and these vary greatly among themselves. Three of the cantonal parliaments are not elected through written, secret ballots, but rather through *Landsgemeinde*, that is a show of hands on the marketplace. This is the practice in the three smallest cantons—Unterwald, Glarus, and Appenzell. In two of these, women still do not have the vote—in violation of the federal constitution—under the pretext that there is no room for them in the square.

The 23 cantons are in turn subdivided into 3,000 *Gemeinde*—municipalities. Some of these units have less than 100 inhabitants, but it is still possible to find the main features of the cantonal level in their political structures. The required number of signatures for initiatives and referendums, is of course, adjusted to the size of the municipality.

It is a firm principle in Switzerland that there shall be no professional politicians. Financial compensation to members of the federal parliament is very modest and insufficient to support even one person. The same principle is also widely applied on the administrative level. Many of the tasks fulfilled by permanent staff officials in Denmark are managed by voluntary staff in Switzerland, such as in the field of education. Compared with other countries, the number of Swiss civil servants is therefore rather low. Civil servants are not employed on a permanent basis, but usually for about four years per engagement instead. Nor is there any fixed system of promotions. It is common practice to bring in people from the outside to fill superior positions.

There is also a significant element of lay people in the legal system. A legal education is not a requirement for becoming a judge, nor is it uncommon in practice for a judge not to be a lawyer. Every canton has its own complete judicial system. The cantonal courts have jurisdiction over both federal and cantonal laws. Judges are appointed for a limited period of time, usually by the cantonal parliament. In cantons where *Landsgemeinde* is the practice, judges too are chosen by a show of hands. Even excluding the most trivial cases, the number of lay judges exceeds that of professional judges. Juries are also used to a greater degree than is the case in Denmark.

One of the most striking consequences of this lay influence is legislation that is relatively simply formulated, readily comprehensible, and easily read. A contributory factor here is the referendum principle. Awareness of the fact that many bills will be evaluated later on in a referendum encourages these relatively simple formulations. A further contributory factor is the use of three official languages. All laws must be published in all three languages. Therefore, it is pointless to develop a special and precise bureaucratic formulation in one language if it is not possible to translate this formulation with the same precision into the other two. For these reasons, everyday usage is almost the norm, leaving the determination of more precise meanings to practice. The written law is considered the foremost legal authority, however.

Switzerland is reputed to be one of the oldest democracies in the world, on the supposition that the democratic form of government dates back to the formation of the confederacy in 1291. This is, however, a profound embellishment of history, considering that the early centuries of the confederacy saw it dominated by a very small number of powerful groups in the Swiss society, and that half of the adult population—women—first became entitled to vote in 1971.

When the real impact of the Swiss form of government on the individual's actual and perceived power/powerlessness is to be evaluated, I believe that we are overly inclined to pay one-sided attention to the, in principle, relatively great opportunity to make oneself heard in referendums, especially initiatives, and to influence administration on the various levels.

For the possible negative correlation between influence on one's own situation and the inclination to commit crimes such as theft, vandalism, and so on, the age groups under 20 are of special interest. It is among these groups that such crimes usually reach their peak. The voting age, however, is 20 years in all but a few cantons. The groups that are most significant in this context thus have no influence in the political process. Moreover, Swiss schools are less democratically run than those in Denmark. In their immediate environment, young persons in Switzerland do not have power or influence. For those who work, the situation is not so very different. Workplaces are consistently more authoritarian and steered from above than are Danish workplaces.

Besides the generally minimal influence exercised by young Swiss over their own and others' situations, the point should also be made that the possibility for the Swiss to exercise *direct* influence over and in their near environment—schools, workplaces, and neighborhoods—is minimal, and clearly less than that enjoyed by Danes.

As a third point in this critical stocktaking of how the Swiss style of government functions in reality is the fact that both direct and indirect power primarily lie outside of the parliamentary system. An analysis from the mid-1970s showed that of the 300 most influential people in Switzerland, only 15 percent were members of one of the parliaments (Levy, 1984). That power first of all lies in capital is true for other European countries as well, but it is especially true for Switzerland—where there are lesser and fewer restrictions on the influence and handling of capital than in Denmark and elsewhere (see Chapter 7). This placement of power in large economic enterprises and in other concentrations of capital does not escape the common man and woman. Opinion polls show that a large proportion of the population believe that Switzerland is ruled more by capital than by the parliaments (*Der Schweizer*, 1983).

Fourth, the parliamentary opportunities are being used by a rather limited and steadily declining proportion of the population. Fewer than 50 percent of eligible voters voted in the most recent federal parliamentary election, and the latest initiatives have on the average attracted only 35 percent. It is not unusual for less than one-fourth of the eligible voters to vote in the referendums. There is a widespread sentiment that it serves no purpose to vote, especially in initiatives, in part because you do not have any impact on the media, where the political debate is really centered. History also shows that it is very difficult to change anything on the federal level by means of initiatives. From 1874 to 1983, there were 67 plebiscites in the form of initiatives, but only eight resulted in the required majority. It is different for referendums—of the 123 held, 96 have reached a majority decision.

Power and influence can be used in two ways: to create and to change, or to prevent change and protect existing conditions. The history of the Swiss society shows that its structure of power and influence has primarily served to preserve the status quo and to sustain an unchanging society to an unusual degree. In particular, it is the principle of hearings in the legislative process, the two chamber principle, and the coalition principle of government, which have performed this preserving function. When initiatives were introduced in the last century, the bourgeois conservative circles were frightened that these would strengthen revolutionary forces, but in practice, the result has been the opposite.

If one were to characterize the form of democracy that Switzerland practises in simple terms, it could be called 'exclusionary democracy'. The democracy in Switzerland is designed in such a way

1) that the groups with the least amount of resources are entirely without influence (the young and the 16 percent of the population consisting of foreigners—and until a few years ago, women);
2) that it is only possible to exercise marginal influence over the shaping of one's near environment where one lives and works (schools, workplaces, and neighborhoods);
3) that individuals can only marginally limit or steer the national and international developments in capital;
4) that the parliamentary structure is perceived by the population as an instrument for preserving rather than changing; and
5) that the formal parliamentary power is in fact not used by those who have it.

The ideological basis for democratic elements in the society's form of government can differ. In Switzerland, this ideology is primarily individualistic. The underlying idea is to provide individuals with the possibility of protecting themselves against others. The opposite is a collective ideology, where the democratic elements are aimed at elevating the population in the community.

There is also a time dimension involved here. After the Second World War, and especially over the past 10–20 years, the outward characteristics of the Swiss form of government have gradually been toned down. The development is towards less municipal and cantonal autonomy, that is, towards greater 'harmonization' and uniformity among the municipalities and among the cantons, and towards more power in the federal state, increased professionalism in politics and administration, and withering of the role played by the representative elections, as can be seen in the sharply decreasing electoral turn-outs.

As happened with urbanization as well, too much attention has been paid in previous criminological studies to some striking formal characteristics of the power structure in Switzerland and too little to their *historical* origin, the *underlying ideas* on which they are based, and the *real modes of functioning*. When a closer look is taken at how the power structure really works in Switzerland, and at how it is perceived and experienced by the Swiss themselves, there are no grounds for expecting that this would engender a lesser sense of powerlessness or less criminality.

Conclusion

The cantonal autonomy and the referendums, on the one hand, and the lack of million-inhabitant cities on the other, have not resulted in a lower level of crime or a slower rise in crime in recent times in comparison with a society such as the Danish. This is not due to the fact that direct control over one's own personal situation and existence—which could have resulted from decentralization— and strong informal social control—which could have resulted from the lack of million-inhabitant cities—are not still good indications of an effective crime prevention. It is instead due to the fact that urbanization in reality *is* not less and to the fact that the individual's degree of influence in reality *is* not greater. The lack of very big cities in Switzerland is offset by what has here been called *inverse-urbanization*, and plebiscites by an *exclusionary democracy*, to such a degree that these social conditions are not essentially different from their counterparts in a society such as the Danish.

9

Control of Young Persons and Drugs

There are no grounds for believing that the conditions underlying the rise in criminality seen in Switzerland in the mid-1970s are unique for that country. By and large, they are the same conditions that underlie the increases in other West European countries. Therefore, we will not discuss these general circumstances in more detail.

On the other hand, some of the factors contributing to the rise in crime are especially *visible* in the Swiss society as a whole and especially *strong* in some parts of it. These involve the criminogenic consequences of an exclusively punishment-oriented control policy over young persons and over drugs. Control of the young and control of drugs have taken special forms in Switzerland over the past 10–15 years, but in their *essence*, these forms of control are identical to those employed in Denmark and many other countries during this period (see especially Winsløw, 1984; Christie & Bruun, 1985). What has happened in Switzerland is therefore not unique, but more of an illuminating *example*, one that clearly and unambiguously shows how a society's attempts at remedying problems of the young and of drugs through the exclusive use of *judicial* control measures has contributed to rather than diminished the scope of crime.

Control Trends

The following description of the policy for controlling young persons and drugs is based on a series of interviews with relevant persons, a survey of annual reports, media reports, and the like, as well as some specific studies (especially Müller, 1982; Kriesi,

1984; *Drogenbericht*, 1983; *Drogen*, 1984; Binder, 1979; Hornung, 1981).

The drug laws in Switzerland were extensively revised in 1975. Among the most important changes was the decision to raise the maximum penalty from 5 to 20 years imprisonment. Another change that would prove to be important was that the mere possession and the mere consumption of drugs, including marijuana, became explicitly punishable. Criminalization of possession and use had been the topic of extensive discussion under the previous legislation.

The *idealistic* aim of the 1975 revision, however, was not penal at all, but rather therapeutic. The drug problem was considered to be not primarily a legal one, but a health problem, which should be dealt with as such. But it was also felt that a precondition for successful treatment was to stop the organized trade in drugs once and for all, and that one of the necessary means for doing so was to criminalize the possession of drugs. Dealers should be punished and their profits confiscated, while drug users should be regarded as sick persons and be given treatment.

Prior to 1975, the criminal justice system had been instrumental in combating the drug problem only to a very limited extent. The rule of thumb prior to 1975 had been that if the police came into contact with someone carrying drugs, that person was driven to the closest out-patient clinic. Despite the treatment orientation of the 1975 revision, after it this practice was gradually transformed into a rule that if the police encountered such a person, they would drive him or her to the nearest jail. So, it was the punitive element of the revision that became the standard. The law revision first of all served specifically as the backdrop for steadily increasing police efforts in 'drug quarters' after 1975 and generally as a base for fighting the 'alternative' youth movement (Joset, 1985). The increasing police efforts have included the assignment of greater numbers of police to the task of combating drugs, the establishment of special units and divisions at an increasing rate, with police work becoming more fieldwork-oriented, and more use of so-called untraditional methods of investigation, such as 'police provocateurs'. The courts have also started inflicting harsher sentences.

The decentralized and cantonal organization of the police has led to considerable differences among regions with regard to how, how intensely, and how fast this development has taken place. Police in the Canton of Zürich have gained a reputation for investing extensive resources in drug areas and for going about it rather forcefully, such as making more frequent arrests. The opposite is found in the Canton of Bern, which has acquired a reputation for a more subdued and less one-sided policing approach. This variation in the character of the measures taken in the different areas is probably greater in Switzerland than in many other countries and provides us with a rather exceptional opportunity to evaluate the results of various courses of action within one country's borders.

The hardliners in the Canton of Zürich have concentrated on the city of Zürich itself, and especially on the center of that city. Many of the actions taken there have been carried out in close cooperation with the city government, and characteristically they have been aimed at 'alternative' youth gatherings broadly defined. It has often not just been a matter of raids and infiltration. Police have also resorted to physically closing down centers or hang-outs for various youth groups. This has been done so consistently and so often that this leveling of houses, cafés, and the like to the ground, as soon as they start becoming popular hang-outs for unorganized youths, must be regarded as a special strategy.

One of the most recent examples is the destruction of a complex in the center of Zürich near one of the central traffic junctions, Bellevue Platz, that was used as a waiting room. This waiting room area had become a hang-out for some youth groups. After the demolition of this building a new café, *Belcafé*, was built in modernistic style—for over $700,000. The waiting room has never been rebuilt, so that people are now forced to wait standing outside in the cold during the winter months. Earlier, an artist's café had been torn down in similar fashion and an office building built to replace it; the jazz club *Africana* was demolished and replaced with a new hotel; and another meeting place for young people, *Platte 27*, has been flattened into a parking lot. Physical destruction of meeting places is a very perceptible and aggressive measure to take in such a small and limited city environment as that in Zürich.

These frontal attempts at controlling youth groups may be an important reason why suddenly in 1980 the slogan 'Züri Brännt' (Zürich burns) appeared in newspapers all over the world and soon thereafter as graffiti in many places—especially in West Germany.

After the first rather subdued alternative youth movements appeared in Zürich as early as 1963, the city later experienced extensive actions and demonstrations in May 1968, as did so many other cities in the western world. However, the youth revolt was less widespread and less dramatic there than in many other big cities in Europe. The focus for the 1968 youth revolt in Zürich was a demand for a youth center, an issue that had already been raised in 1963 by alternative youth groups (Kriesi, 1984). The center was provided in the winter of 1970 two years later. It was a small bunker with no lights, no heating, no other facilities, and with little scope for alteration or improvement. This impossible and unusable bunker was shut down by the young people using it after only three months, which was seen as a proof by the city council and others that autonomous youth centers cannot function.

The 1970s witnessed more demonstrations and numerous negotiations for a new youth center. It was not until May 1980 though that a serious incident again took place. The city council appropriated 61 million SF, almost $36 million, for the restoration of the city's opera house. A small group of demonstrators showed up at the opera house with a banner proclaiming: WIR SIND DIE KULTURLEICHEN DER STADT—we are the city's cultural cadavers. It was a peaceful demonstration, but a large force of police approached wearing visors and demanded that the demonstrators disperse in different directions. The demonstrators refused. The police then dispersed the group by means of tear gas and rubber bullets, injuring several demonstrators. Later the same night, several thousand young people paraded in the streets of Zürich. They too were chased by the police, resulting in several arrests. Most arrests led to sentences for trespassing on private property—in yards, factory grounds, and the like—where they had taken refuge to evade the pursuing police.

The unrest escalated over the following week. Up to 6,000 people, mostly young people, participated in some of the more or less planned demonstrations. The police continued to hit back hard. From 1980–1982, several hundred were slightly and about 50 seriously injured. In the course of the chases in the streets, a fair amount of property damage occurred. In the week following the demonstration at the opera house, damages were incurred to the amount of almost $300,000, and a department store was looted of goods to a value of about $140,000. The demonstration in front of the opera house had by now developed into a youth revolt of much broader dimensions. The young people participating described their own actions in May and June 1980 as the 'pack-ice syndrome': a reaction against what they saw to be the big, impersonal, adult, profit-oriented society (Haller, 1986).

Negotiations with politicians and authorities were initiated immediately, and within a month—28 June 1980—the AJZ, *Auto-nomes Jugend Zentrum* (Autonomus Youth Center), was opened, near the central railway station in Zürich. It was to be a self-governing youth center offering diverse activities. The city that had decided to invest $35 million to restore its opera house, appropriated less than $30,000 to restore the AJZ. The opening of the AJZ was strongly criticized from several quarters, not least of all by the leading conservative newspaper, *Neue Zürcher Zeitung*. It maintained that the AJZ was a center for drug sales. The young people themselves agreed at the start that smoking hashish would be allowed in the house, but that it would be forbidden to sell or use hard drugs.

The police raided the AJZ several times in July and August. After one of the raids, the police filed a report claiming that 'some grams of powder resembling heroin' had been found. It was never determined whether it was really heroin or not, but this incident led to the closing of AJZ on 4 September.

Thereafter followed what has been called 'dem heissen Winter' (the hot winter) with extensive street fighting between the young people and the police. It was during this period in particular that many young people passed 'the point of no return'. They began to see themselves as so criminalized by the police—and thereby rejected by the Swiss society—that they could no longer envisage any future except one in which they joined forces with other 'criminals'. Above all the young drug users felt that this rejection and the chasm between them and the established adult world was enormous and 'final'. After 10 months of street fighting, the youth center was reopened on 3 April 1981.

The police changed their tactics after the reopening. Out of apparent deference to the fact that the young were to govern and supervise themselves, no raids were made on the center. Instead, greater attention was paid to and extra pressure put on all (other) known or potential hang-outs for drug users and dealers in heroin, hashish, etc.—in part by physically destroying these places, as was noted above. For an outside observer, the result of this strategy was not very surprising. Sales of hashish and hard drugs were moved to the youth center and the dealers thereafter took full control of AJZ.

After a month-long election campaign, which focussed on the youth movement and the youth center, a new city council was elected in Zürich in early March, 1982. The election turned out to be a great success for the conservative parties. The election results were described in the newspapers under the headline, *Bewegung machte Zürich bürgerlich* (The youth movement made Zürich conservative). It was during and along with this campaign that the police intensified their efforts against hang-outs and potential spots for drug-dealing. The following description is found in the annual police report for 1982: 'Because of an increase in the number of severe cases of drug-dealing and drug addiction, special police patrols were established and used against all known places for drug use and drug-dealing in the city' (author's translation).

The police commissioner in Zürich contacted the mayor of the newly elected city council in March and proposed that the youth center be demolished. This was done on 23 March 1982, and was thus one of the first official acts of the new council.

Today there is no trace left of the events that took place in Zürich in 1980–1982. Zürich is not 'burning' anymore, and it resembles the pre-1980 Zürich. The area behind the central station near the *Schweizerische Landesmuseum* (National Museum of Switzerland), on Limmatstrasse 20 where the AJZ was situated, is an empty lot overgrown with weeds and wild bushes. The new meeting place for drug users is out-of-doors, along the banks of the Limmat River and the Lake of Zürich.

One of the direct and visible consequences of this control policy of dismantling meeting areas and making frequent arrests is, of course, that drug users have to an even greater degree been concentrated in places reserved for them and a number of others, that is, in the *prisons*. One-third of all the prisoners in Switzerland on any given day in 1983 were there for drug crimes. The drug policy is one of the main reasons why the pressure on the prisons became so much more intense from 1980 to 1983 that the statistics are entitled: *Gefängnisse: alles ausgebucht!* (Prisons: all full up!) (*Gefängnisse*, 1985). Those who are convicted for drug crimes predominate both numerically and even more in length of sentence, since drug sentences are relatively harsh. Whereas only 5 percent of all unconditional custody sentences in Switzerland in 1983 were for longer than one-year's imprisonment, this was true for one-fourth of the drug sentences.

The relatively harsh drug sentences are also evidenced by the fact that while 'only' every eighth prisoner had been convicted for drug crimes, every third prisoner on any given day was serving a sentence for such crimes. If one takes the total sentences to imprisonment in years as a yardstick, there was a rise of 40 percent from 1980 to 1983 in Switzerland.

However, the similarities dominate when Denmark and Switzerland are compared as to sentences, the number of prisons, the prison's organization and methods, the number of prisoners, and so on, both in general and in relation to drugs. In 1984, there were about 70 prisoners in Swiss prisons per 100,000 inhabitants, including pretrial detainees. This level is very close to that of Denmark.

Another direct consequence of the policies for controlling young people and the attention that the issue has received is that youth and drug problems have taken a prominent position in the public consciousness. In 1982, a representative sample of the Swiss population was asked which of the main problems facing Switzerland were still unsolved (*Der Schweizer*, 1983). The question was open, with no pre-formulated answers. 'Youth problems' came first, chosen by almost every fourth person, and 'drug problems' came second, named by one in eight. There were considerable differences between the German-speaking and the French-speaking areas of Switzerland. Unsolved youth and drug problems were much more prominent in the German-speaking region, where the Canton of Zürich is located.

Indirectly, we can see that the prominent position of youth and drug problems in people's minds in 1982 was more determined by the debate and events described in the media than by the population's direct experiences. When asked what they *personally* were worried about or felt was personally disquieting—again an open question—both youth and drug problems landed far down on the list. Only 2 percent named youth problems in response to this question, and only 1 percent, drug problems.

Despite the fact that the ranks of the police force had been increased by one-third from 1975 to 1983—motivated primarily by the drug problem—the 1983 police annual report began with doubts about the ability of the police to wipe out or even reduce the drug problem. The drug scene in Zürich was described as increasingly concentrated in the 'Riviera'—an area along the Limmat river bank—and extensive police actions and numerous searches and arrests were described as ineffective. Totals of about 3,000 intravenous drug addicts were claimed for Zürich, and it was estimated that up to 300 people bought or consumed various forms of drugs on the 'Riviera' at the beginning of the month of February. The cautious conclusion of all this was that police efforts alone would not suffice. Estimates of intravenous addicts in Zürich lie close to those for Copenhagen, after adjusting for population. Similarities are also found in the total estimates of intravenous addicts in Switzerland and Denmark.

In 1983, new signals also came from more central sources about the way in which the drug problem should be viewed. The Ministry of Health released a report in which the dimensions of and damages from narcotic drug abuse were compared to the dimensions of and damages from other types of drugs (*Drogenbericht*, 1983). The conclusion of the report was that resources had been lopsidedly directed towards narcotics and that more interest should be paid to alcohol abuse, abuse of legal medicines, and smoking. The report refers to 1979, for which it documents that there were

4,800 deaths due to cigarette smoking
1,173 deaths due to alcohol abuse
  561 deaths due to chronic poisoning caused by medicinal abuse
  102 deaths resulting from narcotic drugs

In an official almanac published in 1984 which was intended to give a description of the main features of the Swiss society and its policies, alcohol, medicines, tobacco, and narcotic drugs were all treated under the same heading (*Almanach der Schweiz*, 1984). Results from a study of people dependent on alcohol, drugs, or cigarettes at the age of 19, who were then interviewed again three years later, were discussed. The study showed that the use of drugs—primarily hashish, but also opiates—was a passing phenomenon for a good many people. The opposite was true for cigarettes and alcohol. Those who were frequent users at the age of 19 were usually still using them at the age of 22. Among the heavy users of narcotic drugs at 19, more than one-third had stopped by the time they reached 22. Among the heavy drinkers, only one-fifth had stopped, and of the heavy smokers, less than one-tenth had stopped.

It would be impossible to give an in-depth, systematic, and *quantitative* illustration and evaluation of the drug policy and its effects to date, but I have attempted to scrutinize the Swiss statistics on drug crimes, increasingly detailed since the middle of the 1970s—a process that is evidence in itself of how the problem is becoming more visible. The gradual nature of the statistical reorganization is the reason why the following figures and statistics do not all use the same year as a starting point.

The Dimensions and Direction of the Control

First of all, these statistics can be used as a numerical reflection of the dimensions and direction of the control of drug abusers. Primarily they show the number of persons arrested for drug crimes. The main function of these figures is that they may be seen as yardsticks for the level of police activity in the area. This is in part because it is a proactive area as far as the police are concerned and in part because drug abuse was already so extensive there at the beginning of the period—1975—and the legal provisions of such a character that the upper limit for the number of possible arrests was many times greater than the number of arrests that are made today. The more police operating in the area, the more arrests are made. The increasing police efforts are in fact reflected in the rising number of drug arrests, from 5,725 in 1975 to 13,168 in 1983.

The figures on arrests also confirm that the police efforts were most intensive in the Canton of Zürich, especially in the City of Zürich. In the City of Zürich, drug arrests rose to 350 percent. In the Canton of Bern, for example, the arrests 'only' rose by 89 per

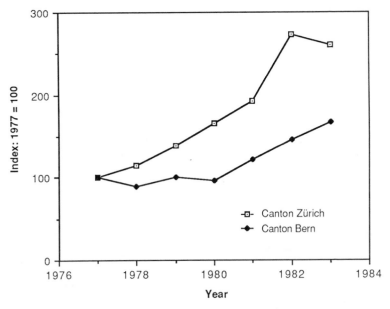

Fig. 22. Persons arrested for drug crimes

cent. The differentials in the developments for the Cantons of Zürich and Bern are shown in Fig. 22.

The statistics can also be used to indicate against *whom* the police have directed their intensified efforts. The 1975 revisions in the law mentioned above were aimed at concentrating more resources against the pushers and dealers who are not themselves drug abusers and who usually have no prior records. The arrest figures show, however, that the increased resources are actually being applied to 'old acquaintances', that is, drug addicts against whom the current charge is mere consumption, as was also the case with their earlier arrests. As the total number of arrests for all of Switzerland rose by 130 percent from 1975 to 1983, the number of arrests of persons with previous arrest records rose by 183 percent. The number of first-time arrests 'only' rose by 98 percent.

Arrests for use alone rose by 161 percent from 1975 to 1983. The number of arrests for offences other than consumption, which in practice means use plus selling, rose by 101 percent. A status report for 1983 shows that the grounds for arrest for 72 percent of all of those arrested for drug offences was consumption, for 23 percent use plus selling, and for 5 percent sales alone.

Starting in 1981, statistics have revealed the proportion of those arrested who were intravenous abusers, 'mainliners'. From 1981 to 1983, the number of arrested mainliners rose by 37 percent, whereas the number of arrestees not known to belong to this category decreased by 4 percent.

Fig. 23 illustrates that the tendency to focus on known drug abusers and their drug use was more pronounced in the Canton of Zürich than in the rest of Switzerland, especially during the period of youth unrest, that is from 1980 onwards.

In the Canton of Zürich, there is a clear rise in the number of persons arrested for drugs who had previous arrest records (recidivists) and who were now arrested for consumption. The percentage rises from about 20 percent in 1975 to about 40 percent in 1983. Throughout the 1980s the percentage in the Canton of Zürich has exceeded that of the rest of Switzerland.

It also appears that the main trends are especially pronounced for the City of Zürich itself. It is possible to identify the proportion of mainliners arrested for drug offences in the City of Zürich since 1973. Practically the entire rise in arrests for drug offences in the City of Zürich is attributable to an increase in arrests of mainliners. The number of mainliners arrested rose from 1975 to 1983 by as much as 604 percent, while other drug arrests rose by 'only' 45

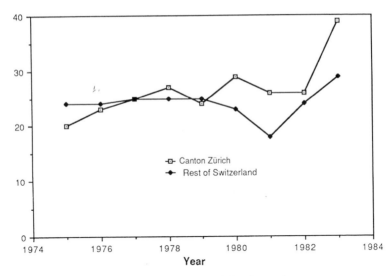

Fig. 23. Persons arrested for drug crimes
Percentage of recidivists

percent. Looked at from a different angle, while one-third of the persons arrested for drug offences were mainliners in 1975, more than three-quarters were eight years later.

The figures for Zürich thus exemplify the general statement that increased police resources in the drug field primarily result in more intensive persecution of the proletariat of drug users: the intravenous addicts. The increased manpower of the narcotics police unit is directed almost exclusively at hunting and capturing known drug abusers, mostly between the ages of 18 and 24 years, at searching them, seizing whatever drugs and money they are holding, and then charging them with 'illegal consumption'.

That it has mainly been a question of increased control of and punitive measures against users, and not against the 'persons profiting from' the illicit distribution rings, is also revealed by the fact that the amount of confiscated drugs, taken during single arrests or actions, has not risen. The confiscated amounts of heroin per arrest are shown in Fig. 24. The average for the entire period is 5 grams per arrest, and the level was not higher in 1983 than it was at the time the law was changed. Nor has there been any increase in confiscated money per arrest.

The effectiveness of the police—in the light of the stated purpose of the law revision—can also be gauged from the proportion

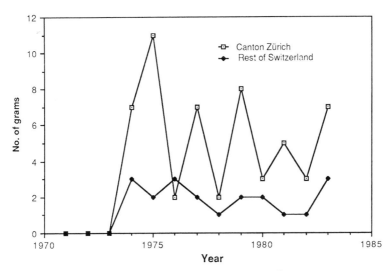

Fig. 24. The effectiveness of the police
Average number of grams of confiscated heroin per arrest

of arrests that result in convictions. Measured in this manner, effectiveness has fallen. At the beginning of the 1970s, about every second arrest resulted in a conviction. By the 1980s, this had dropped to about every fourth arrest.

Impact of Control Measures

It is difficult to prove that the increased police terror—as it has been called by its critics—against drug abusers in particular and against alternative youth meeting places in general, especially in Zürich—have caused the impoverishment and criminalization of these people. However, it must be considered a fact that the intensified control of drug abusers—and thereby of street sales and distribution—has forced the prices of drugs upwards, making the market increasingly lucrative and therefore attractive for drug smugglers and sellers—and thus encouraging the very activity that enlarging the police force was meant to counteract. In their annual report for the City of Zürich, the police explain how they view this development and the situation: 'It is internationally well known that in Switzerland—and especially in Zürich—you can get the highest prices for opiates. This has had the consequence that more and more foreign dealers are attracted to our city' (author's translation).

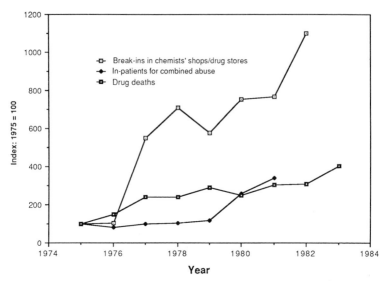

Fig. 25. The situation for drug abusers in Switzerland

The higher prices and the more unstable supply of drugs are in all likelihood the main reasons for the clearly upward trends in mixed abuse, sickness, and deaths from drugs (see Fig. 25).

The number of drug abusers who were in-patients at a psychiatric hospital or clinic for treatment of mixed substance abuse more than tripled from 1975 to 1981. The rise is concentrated to the last part of the period, the 1980s. From 1975 to 1983, the number of known cases of infectious hepatitis among drug abusers more than tripled. Finally, from 1975 to 1983, there was nearly a tripling in the number of drug deaths as well. In absolute numbers, there were 141 drug deaths in 1983 from a population of about 6 million inhabitants.

The statistics allow us to see trends in drug deaths in different parts of Switzerland. As could be expected from the main assumptions underlying this analysis, the rise is particularly strong in the Canton of Zürich and especially in the 1980s. Fig. 26 shows that there has been no noteworthy increase outside the Canton of Zürich. Up to 1977, the number of drug deaths in the Canton of Zürich corresponded to that in the rest of the country, in proportion to the population. But since 1978, the over-representation of drug deaths in the Canton of Zürich has become more and more pronounced. For the Canton of Bern, the number of drug deaths fell from 1977 to 1983.

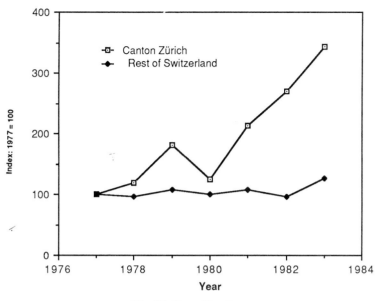

Fig. 26. Drug Deaths

The number of drug deaths in the City of Zürich increased six-fold from 1976 to 1983 (from 6 instances in 1976 to 38 instances in 1983). With a slight shift in time frame, this closely resembles the development in Copenhagen, just as the level reached in Zürich corresponds to that in Copenhagen, in proportion to the population.

The most difficult thing to prove in a systematic manner is the increase in crimes by drug abusers presumably caused by the rise in drug prices. In Fig. 25, we see a huge increase in break-ins into drugstores and the like; break-ins that may be assumed to be committed mainly by drug abusers.

Since 1981, statistics have shown the number of people arrested for mere consumption who at the same time were charged for crimes committed to get money for buying drugs, the so-called *Beschaffungskriminalität*. These arrests rose by 98 percent from 1981 to 1983 in all of Switzerland, and by 207 percent in the Canton of Zürich. Arrests for mere consumption without charges for *Beschaffungskriminalität* rose by 'only' 44 percent for the whole of Switzerland and by 'only' 28 percent for the Canton of Zürich.

It is impossible to determine what effects the higher level of crime among drug users has had on the overall trends in criminality.

As is the case in other European societies, crimes by drug users presumably only account for a small part of the total increase in crime. But the trends in traditional penal code crimes are what could be expected in many ways, based on the assumptions made and the effects of the drug policy implemented—effects that have meant a more expensive, impoverished, and criminalized daily existence for drug abusers:

1) a faster rise in the number of criminal acts than in the number of criminal persons (intensification of the crime picture)
2) a steeper rise in the 1980s than in the 1970s; and
3) a greater rise in the Canton of Zürich than in the rest of Switzerland, as well as a tendency towards greater intensification of the crime picture and a steeper rise in the 1980s than in the 1970s.

Keeping in mind reservations against using the level of convictions as an indication of actual fluctuations in the level of crime, we can observe all of these trends in Fig. 27. The Figure refers only to convictions of persons 18 years of age and older, in this way avoiding the biggest problems associated with using the Swiss conviction statistics (see Chapter 4).

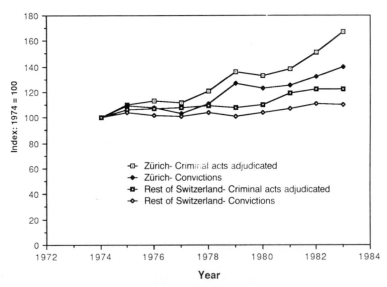

Fig. 27. Persons found guilty and criminal acts adjudicated
18 years and over

To summarize all of these trends, the available Swiss statistics on drug arrests reflect a society's attempt to compel the younger generation into becoming conformistic and law-abiding citizens exclusively by means of legal, especially police, measures, and the unintended but consequential *negative* effects of these measures.

It is important to stress that even if this may be especially *pronounced* in Switzerland, it is not a peculiarly *Swiss* phenomenon. On the contrary, this process characterizes most of the other Western European societies, including Denmark. For those European countries that want to study a system that is different from their own, the Swiss control policies over young people and drugs are rather uninteresting. But for those countries where there is a desire and need to hold up a sensitive and magnifying mirror to reflect their own situation, Switzerland represents an interesting possibility.

For Switzerland itself, the events of the last couple of years have both exposed and given rise to barriers and conflicts to a degree previously unheard of. One effect of this process is that traditional crime problems have come more to the surface of public consciousness. It has become more difficult to maintain the image of Switzerland as a stable society, a society with a negligible crime problem.

10

As White as the Snow-Topped Mountains

Seen from a Danish perspective, crime in Switzerland is not unusually low. Nor has it developed in a particularly unique way. What is remarkable though is that the *image* of crime in Switzerland—both in the eyes of the Swiss and of many others—is so different from the norm. It has become more difficult to maintain this notion in recent years, but the steadily dominant image is one of Switzerland as a country with very little crime. It is worthwhile to try to comprehend the background of this decriminalized image and the effects of it.

A Decriminalized Picture of Society

It is not easy to get a simple answer to questions about actual conditions in Switzerland. The usual response is, 'well, it depends', 'it varies'.

Switzerland *is* a whole composed of many parts that are very different from one another. The most striking dividing lines between the cantons are found in language, religion, urbanization, standard of living, and nature. These dividing lines do not always coincide with each other, as is illustrated in Fig. 28, where the 23 cantons are grouped according to language, religion, and economic conditions.

There are major internal differences even within the main groupings in the figure, such as in languages. The Swiss themselves talk about *Dialektwelle* (the dominance of dialects). The fact that these dividing lines do not coincide makes each canton appear as a rather unique entity, different from all of the others. This uniqueness is

Language		Degree of Socio-economic Development		
German	French / Italian	Advanced	Medium	Backward
Religion (% protestants) — Protestant (57.9–75.2)	German	Zurich	Berne, Basle-Land, Schaff-hausen	Appenzell Inner Rhodes
	French/Italian		Vaud	
Mixed (34.8–55.0)	German	Basle-City	Argovia, Glarus, Grisons, Solo-thurn, Thurgovia	St. Gall
	French/Italian	Geneva	Neuchâtel	
Catholic (4.2–17.4)	German	Zug		Appenzell Outer Rhodes, Lucerne, Nidwalden, Obwalden, Schwyz, Uri
	French/Italian			Jura, Valais, Tessin, Fribourg

Fig. 28. Summary of various characteristics of the Cantons

reinforced by other distinctive traits—perhaps not so crucial to outsiders, but just as much so to inhabitants as the factors above—such as the age of the electorate, the electoral system, the educational system, the administration of justice, the rate of taxation (see also Chapter 8 on decentralization). Added to this there is a historical dimension. Most of the cantons have their own specific history extending far back in time. These differences and similarities in histories may be compared with the differences and similarities found among the Scandinavian countries.

The word used by the German-speaking Swiss for the variations and the uniqueness of the individual cantons is *Regionalismus*.

Moreover, the Swiss people perceive a national uniqueness, *Nationalismus*, besides the very strong feeling of local uniqueness. The Swiss themselves often use the term *Sonderfall Schweiz* (the special case of Switzerland). It is almost impossible to read a daily newspaper or to follow a day's discussions on TV or radio without hearing the expression *Sonderland Schweiz* several times. Switzerland is seen by its inhabitants as something rather special, and the Swiss believe that others perceive the Alpine country as something entirely special as well.

To the question of just what is it that makes Switzerland unique among nations of the world, the most common answer is independence, that is, Swiss efforts to avoid involvements with other countries, and vice versa. This is especially true as regards the policy of neutrality, which has been practised longer and more effectively in Switzerland than in any other European country. The Swiss policy of neutrality originated in the 1600s when Switzerland stayed out of the Thirty Years' War. The policy is thus older than Switzerland itself as a nation state. Nor is Switzerland a member of the United Nations. The most recent proposal for joining was rejected by a clear majority in a March 1986 initiative.

Neutrality is not necessarily synonymous with nor necessarily accompanied by tolerance. Neutrality and independence or autonomy can also be an expression of or give rise to a superior attitude, a sense of being the best, the most able, the most proficient. In any case, it is difficult to imagine that *self-imposed* apartness and a *self-imposed* independence from the outside world do not to some degree influence the self-image, and in a positive way. When one *chooses* to do something differently, it is because one is convinced that this way is better than how others do it. When one *chooses* to stand apart, the reason is the same. Switzerland is not only a country of perpetually white mountain tops. The image the Swiss society has of itself is also lofty and spotlessly white.

The many writers, politicians, and artists who over the years have turned to Switzerland as a refuge have helped to nurture the self-image of Switzerland as a place one comes to, not as a place one willingly leaves. All of the many thousands of foreigners and refugees who have wanted to live and work in Switzerland serve the same function, as do the hundreds of thousands of resident foreigners, who want to become Swiss. These people strengthen the sentiment that Switzerland is an alternative to the rest of the world, a successful 'social experiment'. This success is confirmed by the fact that it has become one of the world's richest nations, almost without slums and with minimal unemployment.

Finally, the democratic structure in Switzerland and the decentralization of the administrative and political decision-making process bolster its *self-made image*, as the end product of the individual's work, diligence, thriftiness, and shrewdness.

These tendencies are not qualitatively different from similar tendencies in the Danish society, among others, and clearly they are tendencies that change over the course of time and vary in intensity among various groups in the population. The Danish society, albeit to a lesser extent, also has its *Regionalismus* and *Nationalismus*.

The point to be made here about the specially strong Swiss self-image and its background is that it would be an arduous task to fuse this image with one of Switzerland as a country with high levels of crime and of the Swiss as criminals. Criminality is supposedly a sign of a flaw in important aspects of social life, thus forcing the admission that the snow is not whiter nor the mountains higher in Switzerland than in other places. *The basic image of Swiss society encourages or perhaps even compels a view of Switzerland as a land of little crime and of most Swiss as law-abiding.*

This characteristic tendency to 'decriminalize' themselves and to 'over-criminalize' others manifests itself in a concrete way in the 1973 victim surveys in Zürich and Stuttgart. There were very few people in Zürich who believed that crime was rising in Zürich, but very many who believed that especially more serious crimes were on the rise elsewhere. This tendency was evident in both absolute and relative terms compared to Stuttgart.

The Contribution of Criminality

One could ask whether it would be possible for this de-criminalized image to survive a confrontation with a reality that is far from crime-free. It has been shown here that Switzerland does not actually have such a uniquely or remarkably low rate of crime. The answer may be that such a confrontation would not damage the image. As has also been pointed out in Chapter 2, crime in Switzerland, Denmark, and many other countries, is a relatively rare and hidden phenomenon—and thus easier to overlook than to see. Crime is not part of most people's daily life, and typically, years can elapse between an individual's experiences of the more serious types of traditional crimes, such as mugging, rape, or burglary. The invisibility of crime—but also the very real absence of it in daily life—causes it to be regarded as *an exception* to the rule *when* it does in fact occur. Being victimized is accompanied by a sense of having been *unfortunate* or *unlucky*. Inversely, *not* being victimized by crime in what is reputed to be a high-crime area is accompanied by a sense of having been *fortunate*. In neither of these situations does the concrete personal experience of crime challenge the image one has of the area and its inhabitants.

Another means of psychologically neutralizing the experience of crime is to place the causes and the actual events outside of one's own society. It is entirely compatible with the Swiss view of their society to consider the non-Swiss foreigners as criminal—or in any case, more criminal than the Swiss. And diligent use is made of this type of explanation for crime. It is in fact the most frequently advanced hypothesis for explaining changes that occur for the worse in Switzerland as regards crime, both on the general statistical level and on the specific episodal level. In particular, it is the *Kriminaltouristen*—criminal foreigners not living or working in Switzerland—who are repeatedly named in the context of explaining levels of and trends in crime.

The Swiss media play an essential role in generating these attitudes. *When* the media do discuss crime or describe criminal episodes, it is quite often cases with foreigners in the leading roles, and often a case of events that have not even occurred in Switzerland (see more about the media in the coming pages, and more about the 'use' of and how the Swiss view foreigners in Chapter 8).

That such 'rationalizations' of crime are relatively specific to the Swiss is again seen in the victim survey in Zürich, where the great majority of *native* Swiss asserted that persons outside their neighborhood were responsible for most crimes. The *foreigners* in Switzerland much less often blamed persons outside of their neighborhood for crimes committed there.

The Contribution of the Authorities

Clinard was able to reach the conclusion that crime was remarkably low in Switzerland because—in my opinion—as a researcher, he was a double victim. First, he was a victim of the American culture and the American perspective (see Chapter 2). Second, he was a victim of the Swiss culture and the Swiss way of seeing things. He was—still in my opinion—not sufficiently attentive to the fact that to an American, almost any European country could appear to be a low-crime area, nor to the fact that merely because people view their own country as free from crime, it does not necessarily mean that this is true. Clinard indulged in this inattentiveness to the point where he actually relied on impressions he got from the police, judges, and professors of criminal law—so-called knowledgeable persons.

When such sources are used, the differences between cantons may greatly affect the reliability to be attached to their observations and assertions. If one generally views the Swiss as law-abiding, and if one lives in an area one perceives as different and often better than the rest of Switzerland, then high levels of crime that may emerge will easily be attributed to the responsible authorities in that region. The conditions for having a low-crime rate are considered extremely propitious, so the police, prosecutors, judges and so on may be regarded as incompetent and ineffective. As one of the few Swiss critics of Clinard's put it:

> Another source of data about crime by Clinard, the interviews of 'knowledgeable persons', is even more questionable. The criteria by which these thirty-five 'wise men' have been selected are not revealed to the reader, but the determinant factor seems to have been the professional involvement in crime-related issues and, it seems, on the 'establishment' side only. Nobody should be seriously surprised to learn that a deputy prosecutor of Geneva, whom you cannot blame for claiming he is doing a good job, thinks that crime rates are much lower in Geneva than in nearby France and that delinquency is often imported from across the border by more criminal neighbors (Cassani, 1984).

There are several means by which the judicial authorities, especially the police, can further this image of themselves as effective by depicting their area of operations as one of low crime. One method is not to record the crimes that come to their attention. There is no doubt that the Swiss police record far fewer thefts and other known crimes than do police in countries like Denmark and West Germany (see Chapter 6).

Another method is to be very restrictive and selective in the information that is published, or even to withhold information on criminal episodes from the general public. All information from the Zürich police to the public is released via a public relations agent, who holds regular weekly press conferences about the general situation. When special events occur, extraordinary conferences are held. These press conferences and this PR agent are the only channels of information for the public on these matters. When a serious crime is committed, it is always only the local police that are sent to investigate at first, thus arousing the least possible attention. Only if the local police find it absolutely necessary to do so, are greater forces sent out. Marked police cars and/or sirens are rarely if ever used. Police vans have two radio channels, one coded and one uncoded. If anything of special interest occurs, the coded channel is the one used. Listening to the police radio then is of no help to the curious public. In the case of homicides, the police declare a black-out in the press for at least 24 hours. Nor is it certain that homicides will be reported in the newspapers. The decision lies very much in the hands of the police.

The Contribution of the Media

Judging from the overall picture, it seems to be the police who almost exclusively use the media in Switzerland and not vice versa. How the media report crime is especially interesting, because it is from exposure to the media that most people form their notions about the nature and volume of and trends in crime. It would be very difficult for a country like Denmark with its daily tabloids to maintain a self-image as a country with little crime. Switzerland has no such newspapers, so its daily readership is not bombarded with challenges to the established view of Switzerland as a land without crime.

The Swiss newspapers print almost no crime stories. No one seems to be able to explain why this is the case. The lack of crime is often given as the reason. But this is arguing in a circle, since people believe that there is not much crime because reports of it so seldom appear in the newspapers. In addition, even if one accepts that the crime rate is relatively low in Switzerland—for example, only one-fourth as high as in Denmark—there would still be plenty of episodes with which to fill the newspapers if that was what the people wanted. The lack of crime stories in the newspapers is a journalistic and editorial choice.

When asked about this editorial choice, many journalists spontaneously responded that not many crime stories are published in the Soviet Union either. In both countries the reasons may be based on a philosophy not to display openly the sores on the body of the society. It is undoubtedly the case—and a logical extension of the Swiss's image of themselves as efficient and 'white'—that criminality is often seen as an open sore, a defect in society that is in part self-imposed. Therefore, discussing and displaying criminality is just not done, not 'comme il faut'. These norms have made strong in-roads among journalists as well as among readers. Crime stories are not as 'good copy' here as they are in so many other countries.

It is important here to understand that it is only traditional crime and related social problems that are excluded from the newspaper columns. Switzerland does have non-subscription newspapers similar to the Danish tabloids. The biggest Swiss tabloid is named *Blick* (Look) and is modelled on the West German *Bild* (Picture). Traditionally and universally four main editorial ingredients grace the pages of such newspapers: sports, sex, celebrity gossip, and crime. The Swiss newspaper has the sports, the sex (including a 'page three pin-up' and advertisements for prostitution), and stories about celebrities in abundance. It is only crime stories that are missing from *Blick*. Frequently nothing appears about crime in *Blick*, and a long time can pass between crime headlines. On 24 February 1986, *Blick* reported that two days earlier a 61-year-old antique dealer had fired 19 shots from two pistols killing his former wife, her new husband, and their son—in a short notice in the lower left-hand corner on the last page in the second section. It is unthinkable that such a story would not have filled the front pages of the tabloids in other countries, at least in Denmark. A story on new military uniforms was given four times as much column space on the same page as the shooting episode under the caption: *Die Soldaten Können auf die neuen Uniformen stolz sein.* (The soldiers can be proud of their new uniforms.)

The other two leading newspapers in the German-speaking part of Switzerland are the *Neue Zürcher Zeitung* and the *Tages Anzeiger*. There is even less crime coverage in these Swiss newspapers than in *Blick*. Nor does television or radio report much crime if the month when I followed and analyzed the reportages in the media is representative.

The editors-in-chief of the Swiss newspapers enjoy absolute power. When a journalist agrees to take on a job, he or she must sign an agreement giving the editor-in-chief the right to refuse any unwanted article without having to justify such a decision. All articles must be approved by the editor-in-chief. It is the editor alone who edits the newspaper, and not an editorial committee.

Some years ago, *Blick* ran a 'rape wave' series, with long, regular articles, big headlines, and photographs. This journalistic style quickly became the subject of widespread and harsh criticism from all over the Swiss media world—including television and radio. The campaign was led by *Neue Zürcher Zeitung*, which with its international standing is the most powerful Swiss newspaper. The other editors-in-chief exerted personal pressure on the chief editor at *Blick*, who succumbed to the pressure and ordered the journalists to stop the series. Since then everyone has kept a low profile with regard to crime stories. Sex, however, does not elicit the same type of reaction, so the response to crime series cannot merely be attributed to a general puritanism.

In this way, the Swiss society affords proof that there is no natural relationship between the level of criminality and the volume of crime stories in the newspapers. The volume of crime stories in Swiss newspapers is the result of an editorial decision—as is also the case in Denmark for instance. The Swiss society thus demonstrates that newspapers—including tabloids—can be sold and read with a minimal of crime coverage.

One potential problem with this limited access to information about crime is the accompanying—or perhaps consequential—lack of close scrutiny of the judicial system. The important role as a critical observer of the judicial system which the media can—and should—play in a democratic society is curbed in Switzerland. It is largely the judicial system itself and its representatives who 'decide' how much and what will appear in the Swiss newspapers on judicial matters. Editors-in-chief and police commissioners normally enjoy a personal and harmonious relationship with each other. Criticisms of the police in the media are rare. *When* they do appear, such as in cases of police violence, the consistent policy of the police has been to decline to comment out of deference to the pending hearing, and after a verdict has been reached, to decline to comment out of deference to the fact that the court had ruled in the case.

The fact that the media to a lesser extent and in a less critical way aim the public spotlight on the functioning of the judicial system in Switzerland may result in greater *possibilities* to 'get away with' various forms of abuse of power. It is impossible to gauge whether this is in fact the case. Some of the known cases of abuse of power may lend support to the notion that a more persistent or critical press coverage would have led to a different outcome. One example is when a cantonal chief constable ordered the installation of secret microphones in a room at police headquarters which was used for consultations between defense attorneys and their clients. Even when the illegality of this was acknowledged, nothing happened.

However, the limited space allotted to crime in the media has in all likelihood also had some benefits. Switzerland's laws and rules concerning press ethics on crime stories (printing photographs of suspects, revealing names of defendants, and so on) are presumably the most restrictive in Europe. Furthermore, the absence of crime stories does tend to assure readers, listeners, and watchers, that crime is rare and a minimal problem in Switzerland, which probably in turn leads to a lower degree of *fear of crime.*

Clinard's 1973 study of Zürich revealed a low level of individual anxiety about crime, in absolute terms. Only 9 percent of the population listed crime as one of the 5 most important current problems. Only 1 percent named crime as *the* most important problem. Much higher priority was given to traffic (see Chapter 3), housing, and environmental problems. Compared to Stuttgart, which had a crime rate similar to that of Zürich (see Chapter 6), the fear of crime was less in Zürich in 1973 (Stephan, 1982). See Fig. 29.

No surveys on the fear of crime that are comparable with those made in other countries have been conducted in Switzerland since 1973. In an interview survey from 1982, only 5 percent responded to an open question that crime was something that personally frightened or worried them. The same percentage mentioned nuclear power and a much larger percentage listed unemployment and environmental problems (*Der Schweizer*, 1983). Compared with Danish surveys, crime seemed to rank much lower in the Swiss hierarchy of personal worries in 1982, both absolutely and

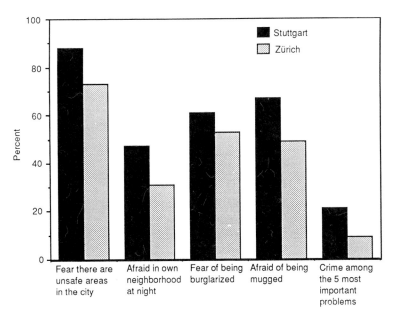

Fig. 29. Fear of crime in Stuttgart and Zürich 1973

relatively. To base something on one's own personal experiences and on more casuistic experiences is problematic. The way in which the fear of crime is expressed is culturally determined, and representatives of other cultures can easily misunderstand certain reactions. An illustration of this is provided by an American criminologist who attended a European conference on criminology a few years ago and claimed to have seen evidence of a high level of fear of crime during his early morning jog through Strasbourg. What he had seen was a number of houses with their window shutters drawn, a normal precaution taken against the heat in warmer climates.

Jogging, though, is perhaps not the worst method of gaining a sense of the fear of crime in a city's population. In Zürich I noticed that people were not frightened when joggers approached them from the rear, in contrast to what I have experienced in Copenhagen and other large cities—and not because of more joggers in Zürich. Nor is it because there are fewer purse-snatchers in Zürich than in Copenhagen—the statistics show no difference.

Clinard used both fear of crime and crime stories in the newspapers as indicators of the volume of crime, on a par with conviction statistics. To compare these phenomena is quite untenable. It is crucial to regard crime, crime reportage, and fear of crime as three *distinct* variables and not as necessarily reflecting the same thing.

Regardless of the more or less positive effects of keeping crime out of the media, we conclude that this is both an expression of and a means of upholding the perception by the Swiss of their country as one with little crime.

The Contribution of the Criminal Statistics

A similar double function can be ascribed to the relative lack of criminal statistics in Switzerland as compared to most other Western European countries. If crime is not regarded as a serious problem, there is no reason to invest large resources in assessing it and compiling statistics. The absence of statistics in turn curbs interest in and discussion about crime problems.

The Contribution of Criminology

Similarly, there is less criminological research being conducted in Switzerland than in other European countries, and this may also be ascribed a double function. There is no incentive for undertaking research on what is seen as a marginal problem, and the absence of research on crime problems emphasizes their marginality, as compared to other subjects such as traffic problems. The existence of traffic problems accords better with the fundamental self-image of the Swiss. The traffic problem is an acceptable social problem which may be related to or even be a direct measure of effectiveness, progress, and affluency. It is also a problem that can be remedied by making less than fundamental changes through technical solutions and practical proficiency (see Chapter 3). Criminological research is supposed to be concerned with the seamy side of society.

In 1972, the *Arbeitsgruppe für Kriminologie des Schweiz* (Working Group of Swiss Criminologists) was formed as a sub-division of the *Schweizisches Nationalkomite für Geistige Gesundheit* (Swiss National Committee for Social Hygiene). This working group has sponsored seminars, but the topics and tone have been more in line with the search for practical solutions and the application of clinical psychology. Since 1975, the working group has published a twice yearly periodical in stenciled format, the *Kriminologischer Bulletin*. The same practical and clinical psychological orientation is evident there.

There was no permanent post for a researcher in criminology in Switzerland until 1983. A professorship was then instituted at the *Rechtswissenschaftliches Seminar der Universität Zürich*. The position is held by Günther Kaiser, who is also professor at the University of Freiburg and head of the *Max-Planck-Institut für ausländisches und internationales Stratfrecht*, also in Freiburg. There are other academic positions with partial specialization in criminological research, such as in Bern, Lausanne, and Geneva, but the total amount of resources allotted for criminological research is very small.

The under-registration of crimes by the police, the absence of criminal statistics, the absence of crime stories in the media, and the absence of criminological research can all be seen to be symptoms of a national self-image in which crime plays no part. These absences are also conducive to upholding this image. When all of these absences are operational at the same time, as in Switzerland, and help to push each other out of rather than into the arena, the impact of the conscious image the citizens have of themselves and of their fellow citizens becomes especially forceful and prominent.

The Contribution of the Penal System

But is the penal system consistent with this image? Sentencing is significantly milder in Switzerland than in the neighboring countries, especially Austria. Overall, it is quite similar to sentencing in Denmark, just as the number of prisoners is similar. One might have expected that the Swiss self-image would have demanded a more pronounced disassociation from offenders and a stronger attempt at 'social renovation' by means of a harsher sentencing practice. A harsh penal system, though, would serve to *dramatize* criminality and the crime situation, an extreme example of which is seen in Saudi Arabia. It would be very difficult to remain 'ignorant' or 'indifferent' about crime if the consequences for the offender were radical and drastic. Besides the relatively mild level of punishment, another consequence of 'ignorance' and 'indifference' in relation to crime problems is little interest in the victims of crime and their situation.

There are, however, punishable acts in Switzerland that are not criminalized in Denmark, for instance. According to the Swiss Penal Code, it is a crime to do deliberate harm to the reputation of Switzerland in the estimation of the outside world. This probably says more than anything else about how important the Swiss self-image is to the Swiss, and about how far they are willing to go to keep it intact.

Export/Import

The Swiss society has extensive contact with the outside world, such as in its extensive goods exports. Switzerland is an economic power in Western Europe, but it is more unclear to just how great a degree the Swiss way of organizing society and relating to problems of crime has extended its influence beyond its borders. But this influence is not of nearly the same caliber or dimensions as the trade in exported goods and its economic impact. One could ask whether it *should* be, and the last pages of this book will appropriately be spent in summarizing the special social features of Swiss society that Denmark and other countries *could*—and perhaps *should*—import, as a matter of (criminal) policy.

The exchange of criminal and other policies between countries cannot be compared to or take the form of the export/import of goods. Solutions to social problems are based on cultural and historical circumstances, and are specific to the individual countries.

Normally then, adopting another country's successful initiatives presupposes that these measures be adapted to the conditions prevailing in the receiving country as well as that such correlated conditions are also more or less adapted. It would not be a matter of 'doing it the way it is done in Switzerland' but rather a matter of allowing this inspiration to lead to new solutions adapted to and based on the special culture and history of Denmark, for instance.

The issue of the Swiss way of doing things as a source of inspiration for changes in other societies is two-fold: firstly, what powers of inspiration the *similarities* may possess, and secondly what forces the *differences* could set in motion.

Import of Similarities

The similarities first. One could ask whether focussing on similarities serves any useful purpose. There is nothing new about similarities and uniformity. On reading the first draft of this book, many of my colleagues offered useful feedback on just this point. They often wrote in the margin alongside descriptions of conditions in Switzerland, 'just like it is in Denmark'. And it is true that in many cases, the facts could apply to both Switzerland and Denmark, and, no doubt, to a lot of other countries. The Swiss do many things in the same was as Danes do. The Swiss society resembles the Danish society in many ways. However, it is often easier to see the faults of others. That is why similarities between Denmark and Switzerland may be useful. There are many things done the same way in Denmark and in Switzerland, but it is easier to see what is done when 'Switzerland' heads the page. It is easier to see what is done and what the effects are in Switzerland than in Denmark, as regards certain specific conditions. Most striking are the similarities between the control structures in Switzerland and Denmark as they are described in Chapters 7, 8, and 9.

Despite the existence of subtle differences between the two countries, the underlying control structures over and regulation of the top and bottom strata of society (see Chapter 8) are of the same, in my opinion, deeply unjust, nature, resulting in, on the one hand, an intense supervision and control of the lowest and most resourceless elements in society (including a policy allowing the export of social problems and perhaps intensification of such problems in countries other than Switzerland) and, on the other hand, a very weak control being exercised over the most powerful elements in society. A detailed comparison of the legislation and policies concerning foreigners in Switzerland and Denmark show that the similarities between them dominate. For example, the Swiss use of foreigners as a 'business-cycle buffer' seems to be a reality, but is it not hypocritical then to omit any mention of the Danish lack of initiative in finding jobs for its foreigners? Of course, the principle of bank secrecy in Switzerland could be questioned, but what about the extremely limited reporting requirements and the extremely limited control over the register of business enterprises in Denmark and most other Western countries?

The developments in Switzerland show in an unusually clear manner how attempts at relieving the youth and drug problems simply by means of legal controls are more likely to contribute to than diminish the scope of crime. In addition there may be a number of damaging effects caused by this form of control (Chapter 9). What is remarkable about this aspect of control in the field of drugs—with the strong emphasis on and steady reinforcement of policing and penal measures—is that the resemblances to the Danish policy during the same period are tremendous. One can perhaps encourage Switzerland to consider revising its policy— which they are in fact in the process of doing, including the legal authorities—but it would not be unreasonable for the Swiss to respond that the Danes should first 'put their own house in order'. How many young Danes must die before the control policy is re-examined, a policy which through its concentration on street-sales has led to the impoverishment and criminalization of increasing numbers of lives and thus formed a major part of the background of these deaths?

The greatest differences are found in the Swiss control structure for 'society's self-regulation' (Chapter 8). The Swiss society is in some respects more democratic and less urbanized than the Danish, even if the basic similarities are clear enough: both Denmark and Switzerland belong to the world community of strongly urbanized representative democracies. It has been shown, however, that this *somewhat* different way of organizing a society has not yielded differences in the frequency of crime. This must be disappointing to those who would like to combat/prevent criminality by making minor adjustments in self-determination and municipal structures. But this is an important point in itself: much greater and more radical changes would be needed than are implied by the differences between Switzerland and Denmark before any noteworthy crime-preventive effects could be achieved. Increasing the power and influence that people have over their own existence and increasing the mutually meaningful interdependence between people by means of democratization and modifications in the urban structure are still viable means of preventing crime—but the changes must be substantial and perceptible.

Import of Differences

The greatest and clearest difference between Switzerland and Denmark is to be found in the self-images of the two countries with regard to crime. Examining the Swiss society provides us with no patent answers or guidelines for diminishing the level of crime, but it does prove that it is possible *to live with crime in a way that is different—and less dramatic—than in Denmark and most other Western countries*. There are three aspects of the Swiss self-image about crime and its background that are worth a closer look.

The first aspect is the reserve with which any intervention is made into the lives of children and young persons who have committed crimes (except drug offences). Prison sentences are not used for persons under 18 years of age, and none of the sanctions that can be meted out to children or young persons may be recorded in the criminal register. Even if formally lower, the age of criminal responsibility in Switzerland is in practice 18 years. The development and future opportunities of children and young persons are not to be jeopardized by entering their names into the criminal register. Moreover, the fact that crimes by children and young persons are not different, and have not developed differently in Switzerland and Denmark, supports the notion that there would be little risk attached to raising the age of criminal responsibility in a country like Denmark from 15 to 18 years. In any case, it should be feasible to restrict prison sentences to adults. We are already well aware that such sentences are especially damaging to young persons.

Second, the scope and intensity of the discussion in Switzerland about some social problems are more proportionate to the objective dimensions of these problems than is the case in Denmark. Far more people are physically injured in traffic accidents than by violence, so that objectively it would be more important to attend to and debate traffic problems. This is what happens in the Swiss media and in the political and judicial arenas there—both in absolute and relative terms.

Third, Switzerland is a concrete example of how some of the most unpleasant side-effects of crime can be substantially reduced:

those of fear and insecurity. The dimensions and intensity of the fear of crime in a society are not only related to the level and character of crime, but also to how the authorities and the media *choose* to present criminality to the population. In Switzerland the choice has been made to give crime a much lower priority on the public agenda than is the case in most other Western countries. There is less public debate about crime and less space allotted to it in the newspapers. The result of this is a quality of life in the big cities in Switzerland not tainted by an ever-present sense of insecurity for as many people or to such an extremely intrusive extent as in corresponding cities in Denmark and many other countries.

A typical defense put forward by politicians and journalists in Denmark when they are criticized for concentrating on crimes such as violence, thefts, and vandalism is that in doing so they are only reflecting reality. Ironically, this is exactly the same argument that is used in Switzerland. When the Danish practice is compared to the Swiss, what is striking is how very untenable—though often well-meaning—this attempt at objectivizing the political and media practice is. It is by choice that politicians and the media focus on crime, and this choice in part also influences the priority that is given to other social problems and in part affects the sense of security in the everyday life of the population, which is perhaps its most direct consequence. Do we not pay too high a price for this in the form of problems that do not receive enough attention and in the form of the mental discomfort and social isolation of many thousands of people resulting from the forced and sensationalistic *non-Swiss* method of relating to and discussing violence, vandalism, and the like? It cannot even be shown that this method has led to any exceptional or noteworthy methods for preventing crime.

References

Adler, Freda. 1983. *Nations Not Obsessed with Crime*. Littleton, Colorado: Fred B. Rothman & Co.

Alles über die Schweiz. Schweizer Almanach. 1984. 6th ed. Transbooks AG, Baden.

Almanach der Schweiz. Daten und Kommentare zu Bevölkerung, Gesellschaft und Politik. 1984. Published by Soziologischen Institut der Universität Zürich, Peter Lang, Bern/Frankfurt am Main/Las Vegas.

Andersen, O. E. 1985. *Risikoen for kriminalitet*. AIM-Nyt, 12 July.

Bachmann, Urs et al. 1985. *Drogenabhängige im Strafvollzug. Sondereinrichtungen?* Verlag Schweizerische Fachstelle für Alkoholprobleme, Lausanne.

Baldwin, John. 1982. Review of Clinard's book, *Cities with Little Crime. British Journal of Criminology*, pp. 301–302.

Bergier, J.-F. 1974. *Naissance et croissance de la Suisse industrielle*. Francke, Bern.

Bibliographie zur schweizerischen Kriminalstatistik. 1985. Materialen zur Statistik, Nr. 19, Bundesamt für Statistik, Bern.

Binder, J. et al. 1979. Entwicklung des Suchtmittelkonsums Schweiz. *Medizinisches Wochenschrift* 109, pp. 1298 ff.

Blancpain, R. & E. Häuselmann. 1974. *Zur Unrast der Jugend*. Huber, Frauenfeld.

Bundesverfassung der Schweizerisschen Eidgenossenschaft vom 29. mai 1874 (Stand am 1. April 1985).

Cahannes, Monique & Richard Müller. 1981. Alcohol Control Policy in Switzerland: An Overview of Political Compromise in Single, Eric, Morgan, Patricia & de Lint, Jan (eds.): *Alcohol, Society and the State— 2—The Social History of Control Policy in Seven Countries*. Addiction Research Foundation, Toronto, Canada, pp. 61–86.

Casparis, John & Edmund W. Vaz. 1978. *Swiss Society and Youth Culture*. E. J. Brill, Leiden.

Cassani, Ursula. Unpublished critical comments on Marshall Clinard's book *Cities with Little Crime: The Case of Switzerland*. Here quoted from Eve & Cassani, 1984.

Christie, N. & K. Bruun: *Den gode fiende. Narkotikapolitikk i Norden.* Universitetsforlaget, Oslo, 1985.

Clinard, Marshall B. 1978. *Cities with Little Crime. The Case of Switzerland.* Cambridge University Press, London/New York/Melbourne.

Der Schweizer und die Grundinstitutionen. Befragung einer repräsentativen Stichprobe von Erwachsenen in der deutschen und in der französischen Schweiz. Schweizerische Gesellschaft für praktische Sozialforschung, Zürich, 1983.

Dessemontet, F. & T. Ansay (eds.). 1981. *Introduction to Swiss Law.* Kluwer Law and Taxation Publishers, Antwerpen/Boston/London/Frankfurt.

Die Strafurteile in der Schweiz. Statistische Quellenwerke der Schweiz, Bundesamt für Statistik, Bern, diverse år.

Drogenbericht. 1983. Bundesamt für Gesundheitswesen, Bern.

Drogen und Strafrechtspflege. 1984. Kriminalstatisik, Nr. 2, Bundesamt für Statistik.

Dünkel, F. & K. Meyer. 1985. *Jugendstrafe und Jugenstrafvollzug. Stationäre Massnahmen der Jugendkriminalrechtspflege im internationalen Vergleich.* Eigenverlag Max-Planck-Institut für ausländisches und internationales Strafrecht, Freiburg, 1985.

Eve, Raymond A. & Ursula Cassani. 1984. The Etiology of Juvenile Delinquency: The United States and Switzerland Compared. *International Journal of Comparative and Applied Criminal Justice,* Vol. 8, Nr. 2, pp. 163–174.

Fahrni, Dieter. 1983. *An Outline History of Switzerland. From the Origins to the Present day.* PRO HELVETIA.

Fodors Switzerland 1986. 1986. Hodder and Stoughton, London/Sidney/Auckland.

Frey, Jörg M. 1968. *Die Kriminalität in Zeiten des Wohlstandes. Eine Untersuchung der schweizerischen Kriminalität von 1951–1964.* Schulthess & Co., Zürich.

Gefängnisse: alles ausgebucht. 1985. Kriminalstatistik, Bundesamt für Statistik, Nr. 1.

Geschäftsbericht des Regierungsrates Canton Zürich, several years of publication.

Graf, Erich Otto. 1978. *Kriminalitaet und sozialer Wandel. Eine soziologisches Untersuchung der Kriminalitaet im Kantons Zürich zwisches 1850 und den ersten Weltkrieg.* Univ. Zürich.

Greve, Vagn. 1972. *Kriminalitet som normalitet.* Juristforbundets Forlag, Copenhagen.

Hacker, Ervin. 1939. *Die Kriminalität des Kantons Zürich. Versuch einer Kriminalaetiologie des Kantons Zürich.* Buchdruckerei Stephan Ludvig, Miskolc.

Haesler, Walter T. 1981. Kriminalität in der Schweiz, in *Die Psychologie des 20. Jahrhunderts,* Band XIV: *Auswirkungen auf die Kriminologie,* pp. 299–325.

Haesler, Walter T. (ed.). 1986. *Viktimologie.* Verlag Rüegger.

Haller, Michael. 1986. *Die Jugend und das Packeis.* Merian Zürich, No. 1, pp. 47–53.

Hauser, R. 1980. *Die Behändlung der Bagatellkriminalität in der Schweiz.* Zeitschrift für die gesamte Strafrechtwissenschaft, 295f.

Heine, Günther & Jakob Locher. 1985. *Jugendstrafrechtspflege in der Schweiz. Eine Untersuchung des Sanktionensystems mit Dokumentation.* Max-Planck-Institut für ausländisches und internationales Strafrecht, Freiburg.

Heine, Günther & Jacob Locher. 1985. *Einschliessungsstrafen und heimerziehung bei jugendlichen straftätern in der Schweiz,* in Dünkel, Frieder & K. Meyer (eds.): *Jugendstrafe und Jugenstrafvollzug. Stationäre Massnahmen der Jugendkriminalrechtspflege im internationalen Vergleich.* Teilband 1: Bundesrepublik Deutschland, Skandinavien und westeuropäische Länder, Freiburg, pp. 317–388.

Hoby, J. P. 1975. *Bildungssystem und Gesellschaft,* Lang, Bern.

Hoffman-Nowotny, Hans-Joachim & Martin Killias. 1978. *Schweiz,* i Gemacher, Ernst, Jubat, Daniel & Mehrläander, Ursula (eds.): *Ausländerpolitik in Konflikt. Arbeitskräfte oder Einwanderer? Konzepte der Aufnahme- und Entsendeländer,* Verlag Neue Gesellschaft GmbH, Bonn, pp. 169–186.

Hornung, R. et al. 1981. *Zürichs Jugend über Drogenkonsum.* Interner Forschungsbericht, Zürich.

Jahresbericht Eidg. Kommission für die Schweizerische Strafvollzugsstatistik. Bundesamt für Statistik, Bern, several years of publication.

Jahresbericht der Kantone über die präventiven und therapeutischen Massnahmen in der Drogenhilfe, incl. Nachtrag stat. Bundesamt für Gesundheitswesen—Koordinations- und Informationsstelle für Drogenfragen, Bern, several years of publication.

Joset, Pierre. 1985. *Drogenpolitik durch Gesetz und Strafe?* Schweizerischer Zeitschrift für Strafrecht, pp. 152–166.

Kaiser, Günther. 1973. *The Volume, Development, and Structure of Registered Criminality in Regard to Switzerland.* Unpublished lectures at the Universities of Freiburg and Basel.

Kaiser, Günther. 1984. *Prison Systems & Correctional Laws: Europe, The United States, and Japan. A Comparative Analysis.* Transnational Publishers, Inc., Dobbs Ferry, New York.

Kaiser, Günther. 1985. *Kriminologie. Eine Einführung in die Grundlagen,* revised edition. C. F. Müller Juristischer Verlag, Heidelberg.

Kaiser, Günther. 1986. *Jugendstrafrecht unde Jugendkriminalität in der Schweiz,* in *Festschrift für Cyril Hegnauer zum 65. Geburtstag.* Stämpfli & Cie, Bern, pp. 197–213.

Kerner, Hans-Jürgen. 1981. Kriminalitätsverlauf und -struktur in der Bundesrepublik Deutschland, in *Die Psychologie des 20. Jahrhunderts,* Band XIV: *Auswirkungen auf die Kriminologie,* pp. 274–285.

Killias, Martin. 1983. *Massenmedien und Kriminalitätsfurcht: Abschied von einer pausiblen Hypothese. Ein selektiver Literaturbericht.* Schweizerische Zeitschrift für Soziologie, Nr. 2, pp. 419–436.

Killias, Martin. 1984. Strafvollzug und Punitivität. *Kriminologisches Bulletin die Criminologie,* Nr. 2, pp. 5–26.

Killias, Martin. 1985. *Crime and Criminology in Switzerland.* Institut de police scientifique et de criminologie, Université de Lausanne.

Killias, Martin. 1985. *Victimization Surveys in Europe: How to adapt American methods to European budgets. Preliminary Lessons from the French Swiss Victimization Survey.* Institut de police scientifique et de criminologie, Université de Lausanne.

Killias, Martin. 1986. *Les romands face au crime. Crime et insécurité en Suisse romande vus par les victimes et non-victimes.* Institut de police scientifique et de criminologie, Université de Lausanne.

Kriesi, Hanspeter. 1980. *Entscheidungsstrukturen und Entscheidungsprozesse in der Schweizer Politik.* Campus, Frankfurt am Main.

Kriesi, Hanspeter et al. 1981. *Politische Aktivität in der Schweiz 1945–1978.* Rúegger, Diessenhofen.

Krisi, Hanspeter. 1984. *Die Zürcher Bewegung. Bilder, Interaktionen, Zusammenhänge.* Campus, Frankfurt/New York.

Kriminalstatistik des Kantons Aargau 1984/1985. 1986. Kantonspolizei Aargau, February 1986.

Kriminalstatistik des Kantons Bern. Polizeikommando des Kantons Bern, several years of publication.

Kriminalstatistik des Kantons Zürich. Kantonspolizei Zürich, several years of publication.

Kühne, Hans Heiner & Koichi Miyazawa. 1979. *Kriminalität und Kriminalitätbekämpfung in Japan. Versuch einer soziokulturellkriminologischen Analyse.* Bundeskriminalamt Wiesbaden.

Levy René. 1984. *The Social Structure of Switzerland, Outline of a Society.* PRO HELVETIA, Zürich.

Mäkela, Klaus et al. 1981. *Alcohol, Society and the State—1—A comparative study of alcohol control.* Addiction Research Foundation, Toronto, Canada.

Minimale Kriminalstatistik. Zentralpolizeibüro, Schweizerische Bundesanwaltschaft, several years of publication.

Miyazawa, Koichi. 1981. Vergleichende Kriminologie: Japan, in *Die Psychologie des 20. Jahrhunderts*, Band XIV: *Auswirkungen auf die Kriminologie*, pp. 1063–1083.

Müller, R. 1982. *Zur Epidemiologie des Konsums legaler und illegaler Drogen in der Schweiz.* Therapeutische Umschau 39, pp. 602ff.

Peck, Dennis L. 1979. Review of Clinard's book, *Cities with Little Crime. Contemporary Sociology*, Vol. 8, Nr. 4, July, pp. 564–565.

Rechenschaftsbericht über die Stattsverwaltung des Kantons Uri in den Jahren 1982 und 1983, Standeskanzlei Uri, Mai 1984.

Rehberg, Jörg. 1980. *Strafrecht II. Strafen und Massnahmen Jugendstrafrecht*, 3rd revised edition, Schultness Polygraphischer Verlag, Zürich.

Schima, Konrad. 1981. Kriminalität in Österreich, in *Die Psychologie des 20. Jahrhunderts*, Bank XIV: *Auswirkungen auf die Kriminologie*, pp. 286–298.

Schultz, H. 1982. *Einführung in den Allgemeinen Teil des Strafrechts, Bd. 2: Die kriminalrechtlichen Sanktionen. Das Jugendstrafrecht*, Bern.

Schweiz 1. 1978. Berlitz Guide.

Schweizerischce Strafgesetzbuch. 1983. 10th revised edition, Orell Füssli, Zürich.

Sieber, M., J. Angst & J. Binder. 1981. *Drogen-, Alkohol- und*

Tabakkonsum. Ein Beitrag zur Epidemiologi und Ätiologie bei jungen Erwachsenen. Bern, Stuttgart, Wien.

Sigg, Oswald. 1983. *Switzerland's Political Institutions*. PRO HELVETIA.

Stadt Zürich. Geschäfftbericht des Stadtrates, several years of publication.

Stadler, Heinz. *The Analysis of Crime in the Canton Uri, a Crime Survey*. Unpublished material.

Statistisches Berichte des Kantons Zürich. Statistiches Amt des kantons Zürich, several years of publication.

Statistisches Jahrbuch der Schweiz. Bundesamt für Statistik, Birkhäuser, Basel, several years of publication.

Steinberg, Jonathan. 1976. *Why Switzerland?* Cambridge University Press, Cambridge.

Stephan, Egon. 1982. The Stuttgart Victimization Survey in *Research in Criminal Justice. Stock-Taking of Criminological Research at the Max-Planck-Institute for Foreign and International Penal Law after a Decade*, Freiburg, pp. 34–49.

Strafurteile 1982. 1984. Kriminialstatistik, Bundesamt für Statistik, Nr. 1.

Tschäni, H. 1974. *Profil der Schweiz*. Sauerländer, Aarau.

Verzeigungen wegen Vergehen gegen das Betäubungsmittelgesetz. Bundesamt für Statistik, Bern, several years of publication.

Wagner, Antonin. 1985. *Wohlfartsstaat Schweiz*. Paul Haupt, Bern und Stuttgart.

Wartburg, W. von. 1979. *Die Versicherung in der Schweiz*. Peter Lang, Bern.

Winsløw, Jacob H. 1984. *Narreskibet—en rejse i stofmisbrugerens selskab fra centrum til periferi af det danske samfund*. SOCPOL, Holte, 1984.

Wyssling, Heinz. 1986. *Arbeit als Droge*. Tages Anzeiger Magazin, Nr. 8, 22, February, pp. 6–12.

Ziegler, Jean. 1977. *Schweiz—medaljens bagside*. Gyldendal, Copenhagen.

Züricher Statistische Nachrichten. Statistisches Amt der Stadt Zürich, several years of publication.